BIGGEST

OF EVERYTHING IN HOCKEY

Transcontinental Books
5800 Saint-Denis Street
Suite 900
Montreal, Que. H2S 3L5
Tel.: 514-273-1066
Toll-free: 1-800-565-5531
www.livres.transcontinental.ca

Bibliothèque et Archives nationales du Québec and Library and Archives Canada cataloguing in publication

Main entry under title :
Biggest of Everything in Hockey
At head of title : The Hockey News.
ISBN 978-1-927632-01-7
1. Hockey - Miscellanea. I. Shuker, Ronnie. II. Hockey news (Montréal, Québec).
III. Title.
GV847.B53 2013 796.962 C2013-941649-8

Project Editor: Ronnie Shuker
Copy Editing: Matt Larkin, Casey Ippolito, Lindsay Collicot
Proofreading: Luke Sawczak
Design (cover and page): Erika Vanderveer

Cover photo credit:
Zdeno Chara: Winslow Townson/USA TODAY Sports

Printed in Canada

Legal deposit – 4th Quarter 2013
National Library of Quebec
National Library of Canada

We acknowledge the financial support of the Government of Canada through the Canada Book Fund for our publishing activities

The Hockey News

BIGGEST

OF EVERYTHING IN HOCKEY

EDITED BY RONNIE SHUKER

TO: MOM & DAD,
MY BIGGEST SUPPORTERS

TABLE OF CONTENTS

TABLE OF CONTENTS

INTRODUCTION

BIGGEST OF EVERYTHING IN HOCKEY

BY RONNIE SHUKER

IN LIFE AND IN HOCKEY – which is, well, life for the hardcore fan – bigger is always better, even if it's bad. The biggest rise the highest when they succeed, but they also fall the hardest when they fail. Either way, where there's size, there's a story.

That's why we've packed the *Biggest of Everything in Hockey* full of the good, the bad and the brutal of the sport's biggest players, teams, coaches, arenas, fans, games, stories, events, legends and so much more. In some cases, like cover giant Zdeno Chara (biggest player and shot), the biggest is simply a barefaced fact. So for those of you who like their truths incontestable, we've put forth some objective ones: biggest arena, trade, payroll, bank account, endorsement earner and crowd, along with a few others.

We could have gone on, but there's only so much fun in that. Hard-and-fast facts are necessary for pundits, but opinions are what fuel fans' passion for the game. So the best of the biggest are all up for debate, which is why the 50 chapters that follow are tilted heavily toward the subjective.

"Big," its cognates and synonyms litter hockey's lexicon, giving a sense of size to matters largely unquantifiable. The NHL is called the "big time," a clutch player "comes up big," a goalie makes a "huge save," a defenseman has a "big blast" from the point, a guy who thrives under pressure is a "big-game player," a bona fide leader is a "huge presence" in the dressing room, a tenacious, undersized player "plays big," an eighth seed knocking off the Presidents' Trophy winner is an "enormous upset." And on and on and on it goes throughout ice vernacular.

Out of hockey's long list of immeasurable traits, we've selected several that are bound to get some blowback. We label the legendary Lester Patrick the biggest braggadocio, the 2012-13 Toronto Maple Leafs the epic of epic fails, Jeremy Roenick the most massive mouth, Rod 'The Bod' Brind'Amour the heavyweight of fitness fanatics, Scotty Bowman the roomiest brain and the Summit Series the grandest of all international showdowns. Of course, no collection of hockey's hugest would be complete without the game's biggest name, Wayne Gretzky. The Great One gets tabbed for having delivered the biggest, baddest and, therefore, best rant ever and being the centerpiece of the most mondo blockbuster of all-time.

Don't like who or what we selected? Well, we've added a sidebar of our top-three "contenders" to size supremacy for every chapter. If you're looking to get contentious with the champion or (in some cases) chump we chose, start with our list of honorable, or dishonorable, mentions. From there you can line up your arguments and then cue the controversy. If you agree with a selection of ours, consider yourself akin to some of the most provocative minds covering the game. If you don't, that's even better, because we love nothing more than to drop the gloves and engage in a good old-fashioned donnybrook debate.

Get ready to roll with the big boys, because the 50 size matters that follow are full of tales about the giants of the sport. And we start with the game's biggest ever: Big 'Z'.

CHAPTER 1

BIGGEST PLAYER

ZDENO CHARA

BY MIKE LOFTUS

SOMEHOW, ZDENO CHARA MANAGES to create an optical illusion.

There's no mistaking the man is big. Among the biggest in any sport you'd care to name. The fact that, at 6-foot-9, he's the tallest man ever to play in the NHL doesn't surprise anyone. Yet Chara still dupes opponents into thinking they actually have room to get around him, like Jay Pandolfo who became Chara's teammate with the Boston Bruins in 2012-13 after playing against him for many years.

"A lot of times, you think you have him beat," Pandolfo said. "But he's got that long reach and he has that strength to recover. Plus, he competes real hard. He's never going to give up on a play. You might think you have him beat, but you really don't."

Chara, the son of a 6-foot-2 dad (Zdenek, a 1976 Olympian for Czechoslovakia in Greco-Roman wrestling) and a 5-foot-9 mom (Viktorina), doesn't like to discuss his height, since he can hardly take credit for it. He has no problem *using* it, though, nor the amazing strength of his 255-pound frame, which he developed while training under his father and maintains today with a legendary regimen of training and diet.

"He's the hardest guy in the league to play against, in my opinion," said Rich Peverley, now an opponent with the Dallas Stars after two seasons on Chara's side. "It's his reach and work ethic. He's always got that extra couple of feet, it seems, because of his stick. And he's also a tremendous player."

Part of it is simple math. Because Chara is taller than 6-foot-6, he's one of the few NHL players allowed to use a stick with a 65-inch shaft, which is two inches longer than is normally permitted. Toss in the 12.5-inch blade of the stick and Chara already has six-and-a-half feet of equipment working for him, and that's at the end of a very long arm.

Size can be a disadvantage, but Chara skates so well for such a big guy, and has so much experience (more than 1,000 NHL games), that he's able to use it to his complete advantage. Because he can efficiently get from point A to point B, moving forward or backward, he makes it almost impossible for opponents to maneuver. Often, players can't even get close to the net. As puck carriers enter the offensive zone, most know better than to try to take the puck across the middle, where Chara can easily poke it off their stick. The most common route is through the faceoff circle, but the deeper puck carriers travel, the more

BIGGEST PLAYER

ZDENO CHARA

“HE’S THE HARDEST GUY IN THE LEAGUE TO PLAY AGAINST”

they run out of space. Those who realize they can’t clear Chara face an even worse realization: he has them trapped and headed for the corner.

“He finishes his hits,” said Chris Kelly, Chara’s teammate with the Ottawa Senators and the Bruins. “He plays with an edge and he plays aggressively, but he plays the game the right way. ‘Z’ isn’t a dirty player at all.”

And he’s not all brawn, either. The big man has hands. Chara was exposed to little elite competition or training while growing up in Trencin, Slovakia. He entered the NHL in 1997-98 and was a defense-only player throughout his first four seasons with the New York Islanders. It wasn’t until after he’d been traded to Ottawa in 2001 that he began to grow the offensive side of his game. Since then, Chara has developed into a consistent double-digit goal scorer and 40-point producer whose record-setting shot is a feared power play weapon. But he became a Norris Trophy winner (2009) and perennial all-star selection by learning how to manipulate his big body unlike any player ever seen in the NHL.

“He’s not scared to use his size, that’s for sure,” said Wade Redden, who also played with Chara in Ottawa and Boston. “That’s another asset he has: he’s a big, tough guy who likes to play hard and make it hard on other guys. He’s got that attitude, that strength, that size, that reach. He’s just a tough guy to beat.”

THE CONTENDERS

TYLER MYERS

The Buffalo Sabres defenseman is one of a handful of NHLers, past and present, that is only one inch shorter than Chara. Myers also plays defense, but it's a different game. At 227 pounds, he doesn't have the bulk to rub out opponents like Chara does, though his excellent skating skills make him a threat to carry the puck and join rushes.

JOHN SCOTT

Scott is also an inch shorter than Chara, but 15 pounds heavier at his listed weight of 270 pounds. He can be intimidating, but as a fourth-line enforcer and bottom-pair defenseman, whose primary responsibility is making sure opponents pay for any liberties taken with smaller teammates, he doesn't have a big impact on a game.

STEVE MCKENNA

At 6-foot-8 and 252 pounds, McKenna came closest in size to Chara. But that's where the similarities end. McKenna, much like Scott, was an enforcer who averaged less than six minutes a game in ice time. He did his job well, however, racking up nearly 100 fights in eight NHL seasons by using his reach to be on the batterer's end far more often than not. His best offensive season came in 2002-03 when he scored nine goals, half of his career total.

CHAPTER 2

BIGGEST SMALL GUY

MARTIN ST-LOUIS

BY BRIAN McNALLY

IT'S THE NATURE OF the sport. Although it might not hurt a hockey player to stand 6-foot-4 and weigh 230 pounds, it's far from necessary in the modern game. Just look at Tampa Bay Lightning right winger Martin St-Louis, who's generously listed at 5-foot-8 and 180 pounds. He's thrived for 14 NHL seasons and is still going strong into his late 30s.

In 2012-13, St-Louis won his second Art Ross Trophy with 60 points in the shortened season, leading the league with 43 assists to go along with 17 goals. In doing so, he became the oldest player ever to win the NHL scoring title. All that came nine years after he won the Art Ross and Hart Trophies in 2003-04, which ended with Tampa Bay hoisting the Stanley Cup. His fellow players handed him the Ted Lindsay Award that same season as the NHL Players' Association's choice for most outstanding player. It was a fitting honor for St-Louis, since Lindsay was one of the league's greatest undersized players.

"What makes you most proud is I had to do that at a time when smaller players were not really taken seriously," St-Louis said. "There were always just a few exceptions. And now it's a trend. It's not about size anymore. It's about skill and speed and not how tall you are."

It's been a remarkable career for a player who went undrafted despite four brilliant years at the University of Vermont. St-Louis was a Hobey Baker Award finalist for the NCAA's top collegiate player three times and he helped Vermont reach the Frozen Four as a junior in 1995-96.

But it didn't count for much. Following his senior season, St-Louis was offered a tryout with the Ottawa Senators and was quickly cut. He had to spend a partial year in the International League before the Calgary Flames gave him another shot and even then St-Louis didn't stick. He spent much of his three years with Calgary playing in the American League for Saint John or sitting in the press box with the Flames. St-Louis had four goals and 16 assists in 69 games over two seasons with Calgary before being waived after 1999-2000. It looked like his career was finished.

Instead, St-Louis signed to play in Tampa Bay, where he figured to get a lot of ice time on a bad team, and immediately took off with 18 goals. Since then, he's passed the 30-goal

BIGGEST SMALL GUY

MARTIN ST-LOUIS

mark six times and put up at least 80 points in six seasons, including a career-high 43 goals and 102 points in 2006-07. Along with his two Art Ross Trophies and Hart Trophy, he's won the Lady Byng three times.

Few wingers have better vision and St-Louis still possesses a strong skating stride that lets him power past opposing defensemen. He's difficult to knock off the puck thanks to a sturdy lower body and he's durable for his size, too. He's missed just seven regular season games out of a possible 786 since the start of 2002-03.

"I know people always expect you to slow down at some point," St-Louis said. "But once you let that creep into your mind, you're going to speed up the process. I have some good hockey left in me and I'll play at a high level as long as I can. I'm not going to let those thoughts creep in."

HENRI RICHARD

THE CONTENDERS

HENRI RICHARD

The Montreal Canadiens' 'Pocket Rocket' didn't match teammate and brother Maurice in stature (he stood just 5-foot-7 and 160 pounds) or individual accolades, but he was a brilliant player in his own right as a center for the Habs from 1955 to 1975. No NHLer has won more Stanley Cups (11). Richard led the league in assists twice and, in his first 15 seasons, recorded at least 50 points 13 times. Now a Hall of Famer, he finished his distinguished career with 1,046 points.

TED LINDSAY

Lindsay stood just 5-foot-8 and weighed 163 pounds, but few players in the '40s and '50s could match his toughness. Lindsay was routinely among the NHL leaders in penalty minutes. He even had 173 at age 39 after coming out of retirement for one season. He possessed plenty of skill, too, playing left wing alongside Gordie Howe and Sid Abel on the Detroit Red Wings' famed 'Production Line.' Lindsay's 78 points in 1949-50 earned him the Art Ross. Eleven times he scored 22 goals or more and he led the NHL with 33 in 1947-48. Lindsay won four Cups with the Red Wings.

THEO FLEURY

The shortest man on the list at 5-foot-6 and 182 pounds, Fleury played with a fury (1,840 career penalty minutes) that belied his size. He never led the NHL in goals or points, but he was a consistent scorer throughout the 1990s and early 2000s, producing 30 or more goals in eight seasons and once notching 50. Only three times in 15 years did he fail to reach the 20-goal mark. Fleury finished with 455 goals in 1,084 games played. In 1988-89, at age 20, he had five goals and six assists in the playoffs to help Calgary win its first Cup.

CHAPTER 3

BIGGEST BLOOD FEUD

DETROIT RED WINGS vs. COLORADO AVALANCHE

BY ADRIAN DATER

NAME THE BEST RIVALRY in pro sports in the late 1990s and early 2000s and you'll likely go right to the usual suspects: Red Sox-Yankees, Dodgers-Giants, Celtics-Lakers, Bears-Packers, Maple Leafs-Senators.

Not even close.

None of them approach the rivalry that was Detroit versus Colorado.

Some of the better rivalries in pro sports had a nastiness quotient like that of the Red Wings-Avalanche rivalry. But when you combine that factor with the high skill level of the teams, nothing comes near it.

Consider a few facts:

1. The Wings and Avalanche met in the Western Conference playoffs in five out of seven years (1996 to 2002) and the teams won a combined five Stanley Cups in that span. Either Detroit or Colorado made it to the conference final in every one of those years.
2. The rosters of the two teams during that period had more than 20 players who are now Hall of Famers (Joe Sakic, Steve Yzerman, Patrick Roy, Brett Hull) or slam-dunk selections once eligible (Nicklas Lidstrom, Peter Forsberg, Dominik Hasek).
3. The goons fought each other, the goalies fought, the skill players fought, the fans fought, and even members of the press from both cities nearly came to blows on more than one occasion.

It was hockey at its best and ugliest. In other words: perfect.

"The more time goes by, the more I keep looking at those years and think, 'Did that really happen?'" said former Colorado defenseman Adam Foote, who played in all the games from those years and has the scars to prove it. "It's hard to describe, actually. The games were beyond intense. You felt like every single second was life or death in some way. Nothing felt better than beating them and nothing felt worse than losing."

The thing about the Wings-Avalanche rivalry is it probably never should have happened. If Quebec hadn't been squeezed by a drop in the Canadian Dollar and an escalation in player salaries in the mid-1990s, the beloved Nordiques would never have left the province for Denver, which had been known as a failed city as far as the NHL went after the Colorado Rockies moved to New Jersey in 1982. If the Wings hadn't run up the score on an embarrassed Patrick Roy and the Canadiens on Dec. 2, 1995, at the old Forum, Roy would never have made his fiery exit out of Montreal in a trade four days later to the fledgling Avalanche. And if a feisty right winger named Claude Lemieux hadn't absent-mindedly signed his name to a faxed contract offer late in 1994-95 while with the Devils, shortly before winning the Conn Smythe Trophy against the Wings, he would never have forced a trade to the Avalanche. In the latter two cases, two of the most central players of the great Detroit-Colorado rivalry would never have been on hand.

The Avalanche's first game in Denver was actually against the Wings on Oct. 6, 1995, and it was a fairly placid affair. Seven months later, however, blood was literally splashing on the ice and the hatred between the teams, fans and cities became real.

"It was probably the best rivalry I was ever a part of," said Detroit coach Scotty Bowman.

Most people remember Lemieux's vicious hit from behind on the Wings' Kris Draper in Game 6 of the 1996 Western Conference final as the touchstone to the intense rivalry, but

> **"THE GAMES WERE BEYOND INTENSE. YOU FELT LIKE EVERY SINGLE SECOND WAS LIFE OR DEATH IN SOME WAY. NOTHING FELT BETTER THAN BEATING THEM AND NOTHING FELT WORSE THAN LOSING"**

many forget it actually started in Game 3 at the old McNichols Sports Arena in Denver.

On a play to the left half-boards in the Colorado end, Foote's head was driven into the glass by a sucker punch from Detroit's Slava Kozlov, opening an 18-stitch gash on Foote's forehead. A few minutes later, Lemieux drilled Kozlov with a sucker punch of his own, which led to him being suspended for Game 4. On the way out of McNichols after Game 3, with his wife and infant son in tow, Lemieux walked past the idling Wings team bus, when suddenly he heard a shout from inside.

"Hey, Lemieux, you SOB," Bowman yelled, "I hope they suspend your ass!"

"Excuse me?" Lemieux said.

Lemieux instantly recognized the voice as Bowman's and went so far as to step inside the bus to confront him. He was greeted with numerous shouts of profanity from the coach and players, still savoring the 6-4 victory that had closed their series deficit at that point to 2-1.

When Colorado came home with a 3-2 series lead for Game 6, Lemieux ran Draper headfirst into the boards early in the game, resulting in multiple facial fractures and blood

BIGGEST BLOOD FEUD

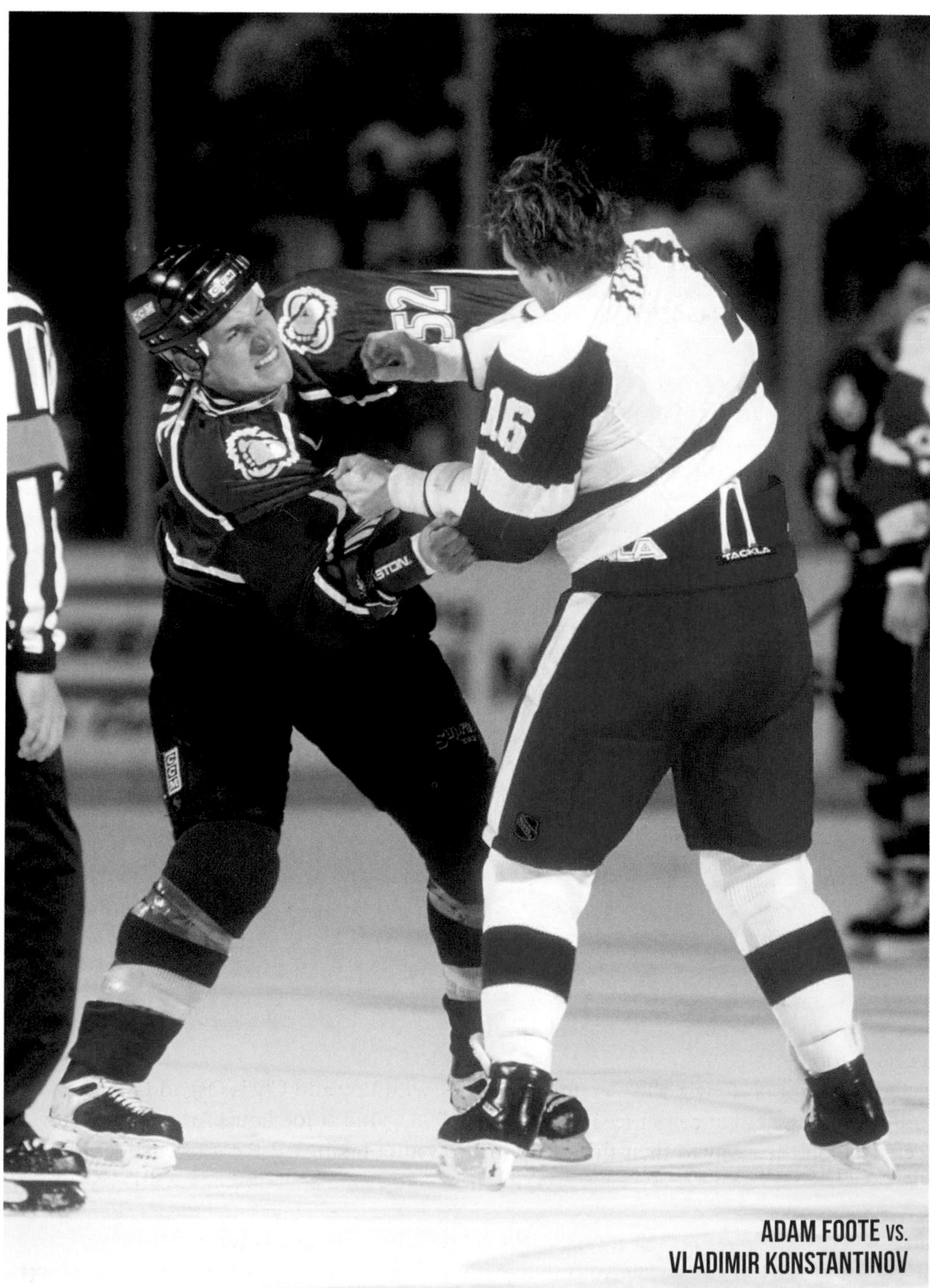

ADAM FOOTE vs.
VLADIMIR KONSTANTINOV

all over the ice by the Detroit bench. After the Avalanche dispatched the Wings that game, Lemieux, who would be suspended for the first two games of the Stanley Cup final against the Florida Panthers for the incident, seemed to shrug off the hit. That only inflamed the Wings and their fans, who hadn't tasted Stanley Cup success since 1955.

"I can't believe I shook his freakin' hand," said Detroit's Dino Ciccarelli after the game, in one of the more memorable quotes of the rivalry.

Detroit vowed revenge on Colorado, but when the Wings entered a March 26, 1997, game at Joe Louis Arena, the Avalanche were not only the defending Stanley Cup champions, they were dominating the Western Conference again. Detroit seemed old and tired next to a Colorado team that featured Roy and numerous other stars, including Lemieux, Foote, Forsberg, Joe Sakic, Adam Deadmarsh, Sandis Ozolinsh and Valeri Kamensky. But starting with that memorable night and continuing for the next two years, bragging rights in the rivalry belonged to Detroit. The brash, rugged third-liner Darren McCarty saw an opportunity to exact physical revenge on Lemieux during a pause in the action late in the first period and he took it, pummelling Lemieux with a flurry of punches that left the veteran dazed and bloodied on the ice, his hands over his head in a meek defense.

That started a wild donnybrook that saw Roy and Mike Vernon trade blows at center ice, a rare fight between goalies that left Roy with a bloody face. When McCarty – who referee Paul Devorski would later admit should have been tossed from the game for cold-cocking Lemieux unprovoked – scored the winning goal on Roy in overtime to cap a 6-5 comeback win, 'The Joe' went wild. Detroit seemed like a new team after that, taking the next two Cups while Colorado sagged.

"It changed the complexion of our team in the dressing room," McCarty said. "We were getting the reputation at the time around the league of a team that was too pretty and not gritty enough. After that game, we felt like we could play any kind of style and still win games."

The Avalanche remained defiant, with veteran Mike Keane mocking the Wings for fighting only on Joe Louis ice, calling Detroit "a bunch of homers." In the 1997 Western Conference final, in the moments following a blowout loss in Game 4, Avalanche coach Marc Crawford launched into a blisteringly profane tirade at Bowman, even mocking the metal plate he supposedly had in his head from a junior hockey accident (Bowman never had a plate inserted). Bowman simply said, "I knew your father before you did," referring to Crawford's dad, Floyd, a longtime coach.

Crawford only responded with more profanity: "Yeah, and he thinks you're a f---ing asshole, too."

Detroit went on to win the Cup in '97 and '98, with Roy and Chris Osgood having another goalie fight at center ice in an April 1, 1998, game at Joe Louis Arena. The Wings were well on their way to their third Cup in a row after taking a 2-0 conference semifinal lead on the Avalanche in 1999. The first two wins were on Denver ice and workers from the Detroit-based Northwest Airlines greeted the Avalanche's charter plane before Game 3 with mocking sweeps of their broomsticks. This time, Colorado would fight back.

The Avalanche suddenly awoke with a blizzard of goal scoring on three different Wings goaltenders (Osgood, Norm Maracle, Bill Ranford) to sweep the next four games. Colorado followed that up with probably the rivalry's most lopsided series victory, a five-game triumph in the 2000 conference semifinal.

After the Avalanche won the Cup in 2001, all the bragging rights to the rivalry were returned to Denver. And when Forsberg scored in overtime to beat the Wings in Game 5 of the 2002 conference final, the Avalanche had a 3-2 lead as they headed back to the Pepsi Center. One more win and it would be four out of five playoff series in Colorado's favor against Detroit. The '97 series would be just an aberration.

But what made the rivalry so great was one side's ability to reach back and land a great punch when all seemed lost. Detroit, with goalie Dominik Hasek, shut out Colorado in the final two games, including a 7-0 blowout at Joe Louis Arena in the deciding Game 7.

Today, players from both sides speak in reverent terms of what it was like during the rivalry, calling it the best hockey they were ever part of. Still, not all of the animosity has died away.

"My stomach still churns whenever I see that Detroit logo," Keane said.

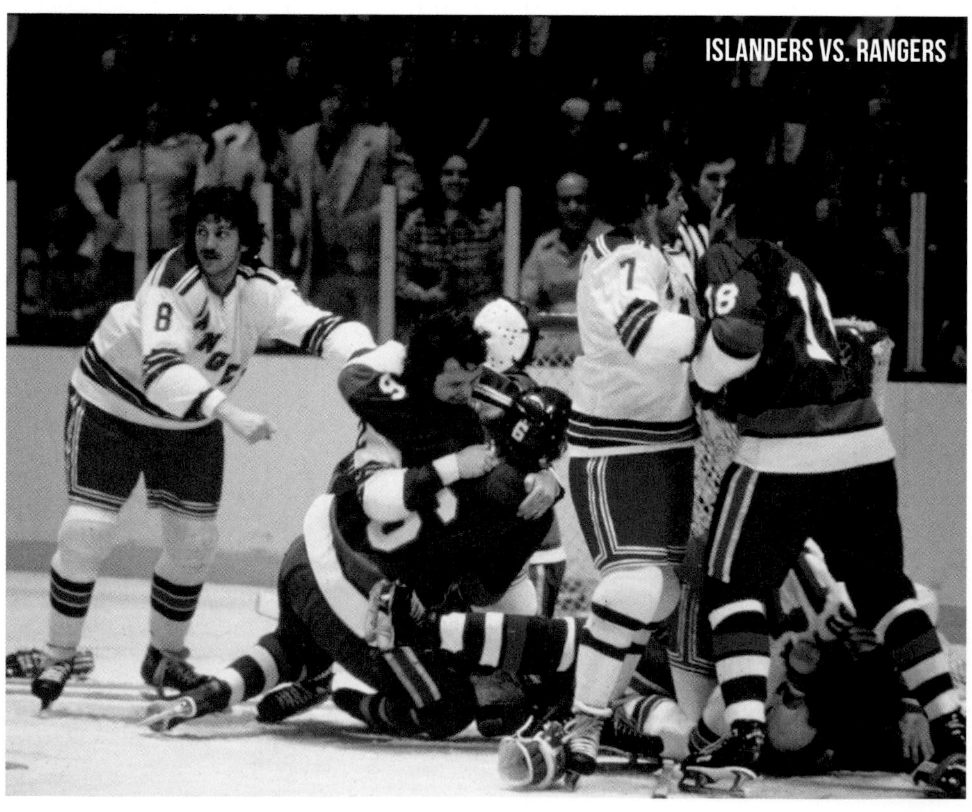

THE CONTENDERS

U.S.S.R. VS. CZECHOSLOVAKIA

In August 1968, Soviet tanks rumbled into Czechoslovakia to quell a liberal political uprising against Communism dubbed the 'Prague Spring.' More than 100 Czechs were killed and bitterness toward the Soviets extended everywhere in Czechoslovakia, especially onto the ice. Czechoslovakia was forced to cancel hosting the 1969 World Championship because of the invasion, which only fuelled the rivalry. When the teams met in Stockholm, Sweden, instead, the fired-up Czechs beat the defending world and Olympic champions in two games. Czech captain Josef Golonka used his stick as a pretend rifle, pointing it at the Soviets bench, and Czech players used tape to cover the red star on their uniforms that signalled solidarity with the Communist cause.

HERSHEY BEARS VS. PHILADELPHIA PHANTOMS

Those who bought tickets to a Bears-Phantoms game knew one thing: they were in for a long, long night. The American League franchises, which were closely situated before the Phantoms moved to Adirondack, saw more fights than the cast members of *The Real Housewives.* The rivalry grew intense in 1996, when the Flyers took their AHL affiliation out of Hershey and moved it to Philadelphia, creating their own team. Hershey, suddenly without an NHL parent club, expressed its unhappiness over the Flyers' decision with many bare-knuckled games. Many contests had penalty minutes reaching into the hundreds.

"There were fights every 10 seconds," said Bob Hartley, former Hershey coach. "It was like a demolition derby out there."

NEW YORK ISLANDERS VS. NEW YORK RANGERS

Come on, we can't leave out a rivalry in which one fan base still chants an opponent's name derogatorily 30-plus years later. An Islanders-Rangers game in Madison Square Garden isn't complete without a "Potvin sucks!" chant. The Original Six Rangers only took the cross-state Islanders seriously after they were upset in a three-game series in the 1975 playoffs. From that point on, the suburban team from Long Island got under the Blueshirts' skin big time, especially after Denis Potvin injured Rangers star Ulf Nilsson with a crushing check in 1979. In a game not long afterward, Potvin was nearly hit by a nine-volt battery thrown from the MSG stands. The rivalry has cooled somewhat in recent years, though, because the teams last met in the playoffs in 1994.

CHAPTER 4

BIGGEST EGO

LESTER PATRICK

BY STAN FISCHLER

THOSE WHO FOLLOW HOCKEY careers like that of Lester Patrick's would attest that 'The Silver Fox' had a right to be an egotist. Big time. In New York, the only pro sports boss with a bigger ego was GM John McGraw of MLB's New York Giants. As New York Rangers defenseman Babe Pratt once put it, "Lester was to hockey what McGraw was to baseball."

Even before Patrick became the patron saint of New York hockey, his accomplishments on and off the ice were legendary. As a player, not only was he the first rushing defenseman, but he also excelled as a rover, in an era when teams iced seven skaters each, and once even played goal. He starred on such early 20th-century teams as Westmount Academy, the Montreal Wanderers and Renfrew Hockey Club, among others.

No single person has contributed more to hockey on every level. After his playing career, Patrick moved on to coaching, managing and operating teams and even leagues. In 1911, along with his brother Frank, Patrick organized the Pacific Coast Hockey Association. While he helped run the PCHA, he also played for the Victoria Aristocrats (later Cougars) and then the Spokane Canaries and Seattle Metropolitans. It was in Victoria that he and his brother built Canada's first artificial hockey rink and then another in Vancouver.

By 1914, with Patrick's guidance, the PCHA was competing in an East-West playoff for the Stanley Cup with the National Hockey Association, the predecessor to the NHL. In 1925, Patrick, by this time 42, coached and managed the Cougars to a Cup triumph over the Montreal Canadiens.

Over two decades, Patrick's eminence – and his ego – grew in proportion to his accomplishments. And as Al Jolson, one of his favorite performers of the day, liked to say, "You ain't seen nothin' yet!"

When owners of Madison Square Garden fired Conn Smythe as Rangers GM in 1926, Patrick was hired as coach-GM. En route to New York's first Cup in 1928, Patrick even replaced his injured goalie Lorne Chabot between the pipes for a playoff game and beat the favored Montreal Maroons 2-1. James Burchard, a hockey writer for the New York *World-Telegram*, was so impressed with Patrick's storybook performance that he authored a 28-line poem about the feat that has been republished over the years.

Patrick's ego was further fed by his successes in coach of the year voting. From the time that honor was first awarded in 1930-31, Patrick was named to the prestigious post in seven of the first eight seasons.

As for his team's success, Patrick was directly competing with the New York Americans (the first NHL team in Manhattan) and rivalling the personality of the Amerks leader Mervyn 'Red' Dutton. But it was no contest. In a monumental clash of enormous egos, Patrick and Dutton exchanged verbal duels throughout the 1930s and into 1941-42 after which Dutton's team folded. Patrick's clubs won three Stanley Cups, Dutton's Amerks none. When Dutton attempted to restore his club to the league after a hiatus during the Second World War, Patrick was powerful enough to help block it.

As Rangers GM, Patrick brought in his older son, Lynn, from out of nowhere to play left wing for the Blueshirts, leading to charges of nepotism in the sports pages. With a sense that his sovereignty had been challenged, Patrick issued what amounted to a royal proclamation – a self-righteous 11-word broadside at the press: "Scurrilous, reprehensible and an irresponsible attack on the integrity of hockey."

Lynn, who went on to become one of the Rangers' leading scorers and a first-team all-star, underlined the point by making the team.

As if Patrick's ego needed any more polishing, on the evening of Dec. 3, 1947, the first hockey event of its kind was held at the Garden: Lester Patrick Night. As if to indicate that, for once, Patrick's ego had been held in check, the New York *Times* reported, "It finally happened to Lester Patrick – he found himself at a loss for words."

Patrick's oversized ego caused extreme friction within the Rangers' organization in the post-Second World War years. Although he'd technically resigned as GM of the Rangers in February 1946 in favor of Frank Boucher, Patrick agreed to stay on in an advisory capacity. Boucher suspected his stewardship would conflict with Patrick's ego and he was right. "As it turned out, my fears were fully justified," Boucher said. "I tried to appease Lester, but he would not bend."

Although he now was only a consultant, Patrick continued to treat Boucher as if he, Patrick, were still running the show. Always, the ego intruded. And when Boucher set up a deal with Montreal that would bring center Buddy O'Connor and defenseman Frankie Eddolls to New York, Patrick went to MSG president John Reed Kilpatrick and tried to overrule the deal. When Boucher learned about Patrick's end run, he offered his resignation, but Kilpatrick sided with Boucher. (That season O'Connor missed being the NHL's leading scorer by a point and won the Hart and Lady Byng Trophies as a Ranger.) At that point, Patrick's ego couldn't tolerate a situation in which he couldn't be the boss. He reluctantly moved into the Rangers' background and permanently left New York in 1948.

BIGGEST EGO

LESTER PATRICK

THE CONTENDERS

MIKE MILBURY

Milbury's ego began growing out of proportion to his ability as a player when *Newsday's* Stan Isaacs wrote that the Boston defenseman was so entertaining, "He should be a between-periods interview at the first *and* second intermissions." If Milbury's ego wasn't big enough then, it ballooned when he was runner-up for the Jack Adams Award in 1990 and haughtily observed, "Coaching isn't microbiology. I've been in the game 16 years and should have figured out something."

More recently, Milbury's ego was inflated even further when he was named an analyst for NBC's NHL network telecasts, on which he's targeted some of the biggest names in the game, including Sidney Crosby and Alex Ovechkin. Not surprisingly, Milbury is a direct disciple of his one-time mentor Don Cherry.

DENIS POTVIN

Sportswriter Bob Verdi of the Chicago *Tribune* once labelled Potvin "hockey's most outspoken superstar." Suave, sophisticated and savvy, Potvin had an ego that was rightfully big. Even his Islanders teammates weren't spared feeling it. At a time when Islanders players lived on Long Island, Potvin broke with tradition and took an apartment in Manhattan, within a slapshot of the Rangers' home, MSG.

Potvin's ego was already big when he got to New York in 1973 and it only grew after he won the Calder Trophy. It didn't hurt that he was almost immediately being compared to the incomparable Bobby Orr. Later, Potvin made headlines by suggesting he was a better player than Orr while playing for Team Canada. "Nobody can accuse Potvin of lacking candor," noted broadcaster Marv Albert.

If that's not enough, after only four years in the NHL, Potvin wrote his autobiography, *Power on Ice.* Considering his on-ice accomplishments, however, he has every right to his big ego. The Hall of Famer led the New York Islanders to four straight Cups and an unprecedented 19 consecutive playoff series wins.

PHIL ESPOSITO

Esposito's braggadocio is rooted in his years starring for the Rangers and Bruins and it only expanded when he got into coaching, general managing and selling the NHL with the Lightning. But 'Espo' is mostly remembered for goals.

"Scoring is easy," he once boasted. "You stand in the slot, take your beating and shoot the puck in the net."

When serving as Rangers GM, Esposito fired coach Michel Bergeron with two games left in 1988-89 and named himself coach. The Blueshirts lost the last two games and were swept by the Pittsburgh Penguins in the first round of the playoffs.

BIGGEST EGO

DENIS POTVIN

CHAPTER 5

BIGGEST MOUTH

JEREMY ROENICK

BY MICHAEL TRAIKOS

SOME PLAYERS RETIRE FROM hockey and are never heard from again. They simply hang up their skates, walk away and let their statistics speak for themselves.

Jeremy Roenick isn't one of them.

As a player, Roenick was loud. He threw thunderous checks, scored big goals and was always willing to fill a reporter's notebook or spice up an otherwise uneventful game. He was part entertainer and part outspoken critic. A rare breed of player so skilled and popular that he was name-dropped in two Vince Vaughn movies, but one who also wasn't afraid to rock the boat and criticize everyone, from NHL commissioner Gary Bettman to now-Hall of Fame goaltender Patrick Roy. Even when he'd lost a tooth and was bleeding like a "stuck pig" or had his jaw broken in 21 places, Roenick couldn't keep his mouth closed.

So it only seems natural that the mouth of the NHL has found an outlet for his personality in his post-playing days. As a part-time actor, hockey analyst for NBC, author and must-follow on Twitter, Roenick has become the United States' version of Don Cherry, minus the gaudy suits and outdated perspective. He's called former teammate Patrick Marleau "gutless" and Ilya Kovalchuk "selfish" and criticized superstars like Sidney Crosby in today's NHL for being scared to speak their minds.

"The modern athlete has become too worried about saying anything that is going to rile up the other team," Roenick wrote in his book, *J.R.: The Fast, Crazy Life of Hockey's Most Outspoken and Most Colorful Personality.* "Modern stars worry too much about being diplomatic. F--- diplomacy."

Tact was never Roenick's strong point. He was one of the most skilled players of his generation, finishing his career with 513 goals and 1,216 points. But you probably knew that already, because Roenick was the type of player that made sure everyone knew the puck had gone in because of him. During the 1996 Western Conference semifinal, Roenick, who was playing for the Chicago Blackhawks, was tripped on a breakaway against the Colorado Avalanche. No penalty shot was called. After the game, Colorado's Roy remarked to reporters, "He knew I was ready for his forehand shot and I don't think he would have beaten me."

JEREMY ROENICK

Roenick couldn't help but take the bait.

"I like Patrick's quote that he would have stopped me," Roenick said. "I just want to know where he was in Game 3 (when Roenick had scored on a previous breakaway attempt). Probably getting his jock out of the stands or in the rafters of the United Center."

Of course, Roy got another jab in.

"I can't really hear what Jeremy says," he quipped, "because I've got my two Stanley Cup rings plugging my ear."

The remark, however, didn't shut Roenick up.

"It was funny, because he says 'plugging my ear,'" Roenick said. "I laughed. I laughed really hard. Loved the rebuttal. My only comeback was scoring on him the next day and ringing out the other ear."

Those types of exchanges are what made the NHL fun during Roenick's time. He was a character, someone who could have been cast on *Slap Shot* as easily as on the WWE. He spoke his mind and sometimes it got him in trouble, but he didn't care. He realized early

"THE MODERN ATHLETE HAS BECOME TOO WORRIED ABOUT SAYING ANYTHING THAT IS GOING TO RILE UP THE OTHER TEAM. MODERN STARS WORRY TOO MUCH ABOUT BEING DIPLOMATIC. F--- DIPLOMACY"

on that sports are a form of entertainment. He took hockey seriously, but never himself seriously. There are videos of him dancing on the ice, mouthing the lyrics to the arena music, chatting with teammates and chirping the opposition.

At the 2003 NHL All-Star Game, organizers were wise enough to attach a microphone to Roenick. The result was something more entertaining than the game itself. After a gap-toothed Dany Heatley scored four goals in the game, not including one in the shootout, Roenick joked, "The good thing is you're going to get that truck (for being named MVP). The bad thing is you're going to be smiling all day on TV and I don't think that's that pretty."

As funny as he was, not everyone appreciated Roenick's comments. The NHL in particular tried many times to put a muzzle on the outspoken critic. It never worked, of course.

Roenick once referred to Bettman and the NHL's powers-that-be as "Neanderthals," suggested Detroit Red Wings coach Mike Babcock was anti-American and openly questioned the decision to select Chris Drury for the 2010 U.S. Olympic team. Sometimes it seemed he was being controversial for the sake of being controversial. Other times, he was a voice of reason.

BIGGEST MOUTH

In a 2004 game against the Buffalo Sabres, Roenick, then with the Philadelphia Flyers, received a high-stick in the face that knocked loose a tooth and caused him to drip blood all over the ice. No penalty was called, despite referee Blaine Angus standing next to him. Roenick was incensed. He threw a water bottle in Angus' direction and afterwards took aim at the NHL.

"He said he didn't see it. What the hell's he looking at?" Roenick asked reporters. "They have to take responsibility for the way they referee. The National Hockey League has to step in and tell these guys to open their f---ing minds. It's ridiculous. It's a joke. Wake up, NHL. Wake up."

Roenick received a game misconduct and was suspended another game.

There have been times – like in the 2004-05 lockout, when he said, "Everybody out there who calls us spoiled because we play a game, they can kiss my ass" – that Roenick probably stepped over the line. But when your mouth is moving that fast, your foot sometimes gets caught in it. Still, there's no question that the game has become a little bland and more boring since Roenick left. So we're glad his voice has found an outlet these days, even if the volume is sometimes a little too loud.

"I can honestly tell you I spoke from my heart and some people didn't like it," Roenick said after he retired in 2009. "Some people thought I was arrogant, which is a little bit true. But I tried to give people what they wanted: a truthful, honest answer."

THE CONTENDERS

SEAN AVERY

Love him or hate him, there's no denying Avery is one of the best trash-talkers the NHL has ever seen. Did he often step over the line? No question. Avery, who reportedly did research on his opponents to better get under their skin, was accused of making racial and discriminatory remarks and was fined six games for his "sloppy seconds" comment regarding Dion Phaneuf's now-wife, actress Elisha Cuthbert, who Avery had dated. But the on-ice agitator was also sometimes funny, like his comment when he was with the New York Rangers that "fatso forgot to shake my hand" after being snubbed by New Jersey Devils goaltender Martin Brodeur following a first-round playoff series in 2008.

MAXIM LAPIERRE

'Lappy,' as he's known to teammates, is known as yappy to the rest of the NHL because of the constant stream of chatter that runs out of his mouth. Occasionally, he even taunts opponents to use their mouth on him. During the 2011 Stanley Cup final, Vancouver's Alexandre Burrows bit the gloved index finger of Boston's Patrice Bergeron. Lapierre responded to the incident by sticking his finger inches away from Bergeron's mouth in a game later in the series.

"(Lapierre) not only gets on his opponents' nerves, but his teammates, too," said Bruins coach Claude Julien during the series. "That's why he's been with three teams this year."

PAUL BISSONNETTE

The press box staple barely plays enough to break a sweat in games when he's not a healthy scratch, but the legion of Twitter followers that @BizNasty2point0 has cultivated over the years tells you his mouth is clearly the fourth-liner's best attribute. From rambling about his parents ("At my parents' house trying to convince my dad to put his shirt on. He has the body of a milk bag") to the hazards of nature ("A bird is sitting on my hockey pants and won't move. Then it took a s--- on them. What the ef is going on."), Bissonnette has become a must for hockey and comedy fans alike.

CHAPTER 6

BIGGEST HAIR

MIKE COMMODORE

BY AARON PORTZLINE

MIKE COMMODORE STUMBLED UPON his signature look – a towering mop of red hair – during a challenge among college roommates in 1998. Commodore, who had arrived a year earlier in Grand Forks, N.D., as a clean-cut defenseman from Fort Saskatchewan, Alta., and his roomies would get a "report card" from coaches that evaluated how they played after each weekend.

A '1' from University of North Dakota coach Dean Blais meant Commodore had played great. A '2' was so-so. A '3' meant he needed help. Commodore, along with roommate Jeff Ulmer, vowed to grow his hair until he got a '3'.

"It went all the way until late in the season and the college kids and the fans were really getting into it," Commodore said. "It became this pretty cool thing."

Commodore and his *coiffure rouge* were just getting started.

He's become known as much for the hay on his head as his play on the ice through an NHL career that spans 11 seasons, eight franchises, two Stanley Cup runs and a championship with the Carolina Hurricanes in 2006. At 6-foot-4, he's always stood out. Topped with Calgary Flame-red hair, he's impossible to miss.

"It would not have had the impact if I had brown or black hair," Commodore said. "It's the one time in life when having red hair was actually an advantage."

Commodore settled into a routine early in his career. He'd get sheared just before training camp, then let his hair climb toward the heavens until the season ended. But it would have been easier to get haircuts.

"I used to have to get it soaking wet just to get my helmet on," Commodore said. "It was a pain in the ass, actually, because – oh my god – when you're playing for the Stanley Cup in Raleigh in June it's 95 or 100 degrees. I was dying. When I played in the final with Calgary, we played in Tampa Bay and that was worse. I couldn't go outside."

Only two coaches had issues with Commodore's follicle foibles. Before the 1999 NCAA Frozen Four, Blais made him cut it because he feared officials would target him.

"He said, 'The refs don't like you anyways. You'll be in the penalty box all game if you draw that kind of attention,'" Commodore said.

And then there was New Jersey Devils GM Lou Lamoriello whose rules dictated high-

and-tights. (Jealousy, perhaps?) More fans might have agreed with Lamoriello if Commodore hadn't turned his chia pet into a boon for charities. He's raised at least $100,000 posing for pictures and getting post-season haircuts for cancer fundraisers. He hopes that – and his play, of course – will be what people remember him for. Commodore had played 484 regular season games and 53 playoff games heading into 2013-14 and at 34 years old he wants to keep playing.

"The fans love it and that's why I kept doing it," Commodore said. "It put me on the map with some people and we've used it for a bunch of good causes. I feel pretty good about that."

THE CONTENDERS

RON DUGUAY

Duguay may have been the first NHL player to parlay big hair into a big deal. His flowing curly golden locks helped make him and the New York Rangers a hit on Broadway during the '70s and '80s. He chummed around with stars such as visionary artist Andy Warhol and tennis icon John McEnroe, married model Robin Bobo, partied at Studio 54 and rubbed elbows with the likes of Cher, Bianca Jagger and Farah Fawcett. Not bad for a Sudbury, Ont., native.

JAROMIR JAGR

Great dos – and don'ts – have dotted the NHL landscape for 40 years, but the mullet has never quite gone out of style. Jagr is the poster boy for the party-in-the-back look, which he brought to prominence in the early 1990s when he won two Stanley Cups with the Pittsburgh Penguins. Other players have carried the torch since, including Mike Ricci, Ryan Smyth, Michal Handzus and Patrick Kane, along with broadcasters Barry Melrose and Brian Engblom.

CHRIS SIMON

Before he became notorious as one of the NHL's most often suspended players, Simon had built a reputation as an imposing power forward. He used his hair on a public platform twice. Simon, an Ojibwa Indian, began growing his hair on the very day in 1992 when he stopped an addiction to alcohol. By the late 1990s, it was draped over the numbers on his back. Then in 2000 he chopped his hair before training camp, a protest against the Ontario government oppressing the rights of Aboriginal Canadians.

CHAPTER 7

BIGGEST BEARD

GREG ZANON

BY TAYLOR ROCCA

BEARDS. THEY COME IN all shapes, sizes, colors and lengths.

In the NHL, they come at different times of the year. You're most likely to see them during the playoffs, as superstitious players avoid the razor in the hope that doing so will propel them to Stanley Cup glory. Sometimes it works, most of the time it doesn't.

For defenseman Greg Zanon, however, the beard he sported in 2012-13 wasn't due to the post-season, since his Colorado Avalanche finished last in the Western Conference. In fact, it was due to not playing hockey at all.

After stops in Nashville, Minnesota and Boston, Zanon signed a two-year, $4.5-million contract in the summer of 2012 to play in Colorado. His tour of duty with the Avalanche, however, didn't begin when expected, with the NHL lockout pushing back the puck drop from October 2012 to January 2013. So Zanon took a playoff tradition and turned it into a lockout pledge. By the time he came to training camp, his face was already in post-season form. With a smooth-shaven head and an unshaven face, Zanon stepped onto the ice and players and fans across the league noticed the change in his appearance immediately.

"With the lockout happening I decided to just grow it until the season started," he said. "When the season started I was too attached to it and didn't want to shave. I don't have the privilege of growing my hair out.

"A lot of people think I'm nuts for growing it this long. I took a little heat from some guys on the ice, but they just wish they could grow as good of a beard."

When 2012-13 ended, Zanon had his contract bought out by the Avalanche, but his beard had yet to touch a razor. It was quickly approaching 10 months of growth and he expected to take it to the one-year mark before making a decision on whether to stick with it. Despite the lengthy test period, Zanon said there isn't much maintenance or grooming required, just some conditioning here and there.

"Everybody has his own style," he said. "I can't grow my hair very long because of balding reasons, so I grow my beard."

GREG ZANON

THE CONTENDERS

BRENT BURNS

Burns has undergone an even more shocking transformation than Zanon. The photos of Burns' evolution over the years since he entered the league were one of the quickest-spreading stories early in 2012-13. The San Jose Sharks defenseman-turned-right-winger even drew comparisons to Chewbacca from *Star Wars*. But even with Burns' furry resemblance to the Wookiee, the beast on his face didn't quite match up to the work put in by his good friend Zanon.

"We both have different beard styles," Zanon said. "I don't know if he can de-throne me. I have way more length."

SCOTT NIEDERMAYER

When Niedermayer captured his fourth Stanley Cup with the Anaheim Ducks in 2007, no one was left guessing just how experienced the veteran blueliner was. The tale was written right in Niedermayer's salt-and-pepper beard. Grizzled and thick, the beard on the Ducks captain was a testament to his dedication and hard work during his career. At that time, Niedermayer had soldiered through his 14th NHL season. By the time his career was over, his list of accolades extended far beyond the length of his 2007 playoff beard, including a Memorial Cup (1992), two Olympic gold medals (2002, 2010), a Norris Trophy (2004) and a Conn Smythe Trophy (2007) in addition to his four Stanley Cup rings (1995, 2000, 2003, 2007).

MIKE COMMODORE

The fiery, redheaded defenseman and his beard first came to prominence during the 2004 Stanley Cup playoffs. Commodore was patrolling the blueline for the Calgary Flames and as the team advanced to Game 7 of the Stanley Cup final, so did the immense size of his hair and beard. Although he didn't light up the ice with his offense (Commodore only had two assists in 20 playoff games), it was impossible to miss his bushy beard.

CHAPTER 8

BIGGEST NOSE

TIM HUNTER

BY CASEY IPPOLITO

TIM HUNTER'S NOSE KNOWS no equal. It looks like it was crudely sculpted out of clay and mistakenly placed on a head too small for its proportions. He earned the nickname 'Sharkey' not because he finished his career with San Jose, but because during a day off in Los Angeles a teammate saw Hunter floating on his back in the water and yelled, "There's a shark in the pool!"

In his 15-year career, Hunter fought 199 times. With all those hours logged exchanging punches, a fairly obvious conclusion comes to mind: his nose took its shape by absorbing countless right hands from NHL heavyweights. But that conclusion would be wrong.

"One time we were all sitting around and someone asked Timmy, 'How many times have you had that nose broken?' " recalled Terry Crisp, who coached Hunter and the Calgary Flames to the Stanley Cup in 1989. "And Timmy goes, 'None.' I would've said 10, but he's like, 'None.' And he never backed off it. I wasn't about to dispute it with him."

Hunter sits eighth all-time in penalty minutes, despite playing at least 85 fewer games than the seven players with more. In other words, he enforced. He tussled with the league's most feared heavyweights, including legendary tilts with Dave Semenko of the rival Edmonton Oilers during his 10 seasons as a Flame.

Theo Fleury knows how Hunter kept his snout intact, having watched his scraps from ice level as a teammate over four seasons wearing the flaming 'C.'

"He was one of the smartest fighters I've ever seen, that's for sure," Fleury said. "He very rarely got tagged with any good shots that I saw."

With such a prominent proboscis, the ball was on the tee for opponents to chirp, but Hunter didn't take tongue-lashings as often as one might expect. And for good reason. As Henry Hill said in Martin Scorsese's *Goodfellas*, it was "out of respect."

"They'd yap at Fleury, they'd yap at Gilmour, they'd yap at other guys they figured couldn't do a lot of damage to them," Crisp said. "But not too many guys made fun of Timmy. They knew he was going to get on the ice eventually. He was going to get out there and he has a memory."

Hunter certainly didn't win the aesthetic lottery, but his beak added to the tough-guy look.

"Look at Sylvester Stallone in *Rocky*," Crisp said. "He's got a big prominent nose also,

BIGGEST NOSE

TIM HUNTER

and you see him in the movie and say, "Oh boy, look at that guy, he's tough." You're thinking anybody who has a nose like that has got to be tough."

Since retiring as a player, Hunter has spent much of his time behind the bench, with stints as an assistant coach with the Washington Capitals, San Jose Sharks and Toronto Maple Leafs. His fighting prowess and quiet leadership have translated well to the coaching ranks from his playing days.

"You could see it back then," Crisp said. "He listened, he absorbed, he asked questions. And all his questions were on the positive side. He never whined. When he stood up and talked, everybody listened. He was never loud. He'd just stand up, say what he had to say and the guys listened to him."

And if they weren't listening, they were probably marvelling at his nose.

THE CONTENDERS

ADAM FOOTE

Long, arched, bulging and crooked, Foote's nose is rife with memorable qualities. It's only fitting that it belongs to a tough-as-nails defenseman whose style could best be described as hard-nosed. He played most of his 19-year career with the Colorado Avalanche, winning two Stanley Cups and representing Canada at the Olympics three times, once winning gold. Like his nose, Foote's game had visible snarl. Every year around draft time, young blueliners with hopes of playing a top-four shutdown role are commonly referred to as the "Adam Foote type."

MILAN LUCIC

Lucic is the quintessential power forward, in look and in substance. Adept at using his 6-foot-4 frame to protect the puck and bully his way to the net, he also uses it to bulldoze opponents and throw knockout right hands. Lucic has used his unique blend of skill and brawn to win a Memorial Cup and a Stanley Cup, while carving a reputation as a capable goal scorer. He intimidates opponents with enormous sloped shoulders, a menacing glare and a nose that looks capable of hammering through bone. Lucic's schnoz owes its current form to several breaks, one of which he sustained in a fight and which blocked airflow in his right nostril for most of the Boston Bruins' Cup-winning 2010-11 season.

PAT VERBEEK

Verbeek was dubbed 'The Little Ball of Hate' by teammate Glenn Healy and it was no arbitrary moniker. He was a model pest who sported quite the (Ver) beak, poking his pointy nose into scrums and chirping at every opportunity. The skilled agitator notched 20 or more goals 13 times and at least 100 penalty minutes 14 times. The result after 20 seasons was an impressive record: he remains the only player with at least 500 goals and 2,500 penalty minutes.

CHAPTER 9

BIGGEST ARENA

UNITED CENTER

BY KYLE CICERELLA

WHEN CHICAGO STADIUM COULD no longer hide its age, it was evident to late Blackhawks owner Bill Wirtz that his team needed a new home. So, in 1988, he formed a partnership with Jerry Reinsdorf, the majority owner of the NBA's Bulls, and together they planned a new arena to house both clubs.

Chicago Stadium opened in 1929 and had a smaller ice surface than any other arena in the NHL. Players had to walk up steps to go from the sunken dressing room to the ice and the corridors were too small to be fan-friendly for those who attended Hawks games in the 17,317-seat arena. Even with the building outdated and in its final stages, however, it wasn't going to be easy to replace the original 'Madhouse on Madison.' It took four years of planning before breaking ground on the new arena in April 1992 and another 26 months of construction. But on August 18, 1994, Wirtz and Reinsdorf announced the transition from Chicago Stadium as they unveiled a massive new arena named the United Center. At 960,000 square feet, it was not only nearly triple the size of the old Stadium, it was, and 20 years later still is, the biggest arena in the NHL.

"It was built very well," said former Hawks assistant GM Rick Dudley. "I can't speak on behalf of the Bulls, but the Chicago Blackhawks do everything first class."

Built just south of the original Stadium on West Madison Street in western Chicago, the United Center was designed to be the leader of sports arenas. The building seats 19,700 fans, second-most in the league behind the Bell Centre in Montreal, but take standing room into consideration and the United Center can host more than 22,200 fans for a game. It has 167 executive suites, 34 theater boxes and five super suites to go along with seven restaurants, 35 food concession stands and 50 bathrooms.

Dudley experienced the atmosphere of Chicago Stadium in the 1970s as a player and in the '80s and '90s as a coach (both with the Buffalo Sabres), but expressed awe with the Hawks' new digs.

"The dressing room is magnificent, offices are beautiful, seats are nice, concourse is lovely," he said. "What amazed me, my first visual, long before I worked for the Hawks, was the number of suites. The United Center has three rows of suites and it was staggering to see."

Although the experience for fans was the primary focus of the United Center, no expense was spared for the players either. The Hawks have the entire north side of ice level as their own dressing, training and coaching facilities. It includes a main dressing room, lounge area, changeroom, medical room, standard showers, bathroom, whirlpool and dry sauna. There are also offices for the coach, assistant coaches and trainers, as well as storage for equipment.

One thing Chicago Stadium was famous for was the noise created within its tiny walls, especially from its famous pipe organ. An updated digital organ was installed in the southwest corner of the United Center's 300 level to replicate that atmosphere.

"It was chilling because Chicago Stadium was so loud, you could feel yourself vibrating," Dudley said. "As a coach, I told my players to close your eyes and pretend they were cheering for you. But they replicated that very well with the United Center."

Because of the 1994 NHL lockout, the Hawks didn't play their first game in the United

"CHICAGO STADIUM WAS SO LOUD, YOU COULD FEEL YOURSELF VIBRATING. I TOLD MY PLAYERS TO CLOSE YOUR EYES AND PRETEND THEY WERE CHEERING FOR YOU. BUT THEY REPLICATED THAT VERY WELL WITH THE UNITED CENTER"

Center until Jan. 25, 1995. Chicago's Joe Murphy scored the first goal in the new arena in a 5-1 win against the Edmonton Oilers. And despite the shortened season, Chicago became the first NHL franchise to average more than 20,000 fans per game. These numbers weren't just due to the abbreviated campaign, though. The Hawks repeated this success when they averaged 20,415 fans in 41 home games the following season.

The United Center hasn't always had the same success with hockey fans that it did in its early days, even becoming the league's second-worst arena for attendance in 2006. The combination of franchise players Patrick Kane and Jonathan Toews, however, along with Stanley Cups in 2010 and 2013, brought the Hawks right back to the top of the league after 2012-13. Even though the United Center was built for the future of sporting events, it has always acknowledged its history from Chicago Stadium. In 2009, the United Center had renovations made to its upper concourse and the building has taken on the original nickname: Madhouse on Madison.

CHICAG
GATE 3

BIGGEST ARENA

UNITED CENTER

THE CONTENDERS

ERICSSON GLOBE

The Ericsson Globe Arena in Stockholm, Sweden, is much smaller than the average NHL arena and only seats 13,850, but it holds the record for being the biggest hemispherical building in the world with a diameter of 361 feet and inner height of 279 feet. It also represents the sun in the Sweden Solar System, the world's largest permanent scale model of the solar system. Known as Sweden's national arena, it opened in 1989 and has hosted the World Championship four times. The NHL kicked off 2011-12 with two games at the Globe, featuring the New York Rangers.

BELL CENTRE

As with every Original Six team, the Montreal Canadiens outlived their ancient arena, the Forum, and needed a new one to fit with the times. In 1996, Montreal moved into its new digs, then known as the Molson Centre. Now called the Bell Centre, it has the largest seating capacity of any hockey arena in North America at 21,273. Montreal hasn't won a Stanley Cup since the era of the Forum, but every game since January 2004 has been a sellout.

TAMPA BAY TIMES FORUM

In 2011, the Tampa Bay Times Forum, then called the St. Pete Times Forum, underwent a multimillion-dollar renovation, which included the installation of North America's biggest center-hung arena scoreboard. With fan experience in mind, a $5-million HD video display board built by Daktronics was installed for the start of 2012-13. It boasts the clearest image possible on four screens with a combined 3,920 square feet of viewing. It takes a team of staff to run the scoreboard from a control room, producing video, animation, graphics, scores and statistics.

CHAPTER 10

BIGGEST FAN

'DANCING GABE'

BY GEOFF KIRBYSON

ASIDE FROM THE ODD player on the opposition bench and a select few on the home side, Gabe Langlois is the best-known person at every Winnipeg Jets home game. Known simply as 'Dancing Gabe,' the 50-year-old has ingrained himself in Winnipeg's sporting culture over the past quarter century for his unparalleled fandom and his unmatched dancing skills. Whether it's the Jets, the Winnipeg Blue Bombers, baseball's Winnipeg Goldeyes or high school sporting events around town, Langlois is there, showing off a soft sneaker whenever the music plays.

You want popularity? Cults would kill to have the following he has.

Consider the fans who gathered at the intersection of Portage and Main in Winnipeg to celebrate the return of the NHL in May 2011. When Langlois joined the throng, the chants of "Go, Jets, Go!" were quickly replaced by "Gabe, Gabe, Gabe!" and he was mobbed for pictures and high fives.

As is often the case, the legend was pretty much born by accident. Langlois, who has a condition his mother considers to be autism, was spotted dancing at a sporting event in the early 1990s by Jets executive Mike O'Hearn, who gave him a jersey. The rest is Winnipeg sporting history.

"Then, boom, I was on national television, TSN," Langlois said.

Just like the players, Dancing Gabe has a game day routine. He eats dinner at the St. Vital home he shares with his mother in the suburbs, grabs his favorite jersey out of his closet (he has more than a dozen from various Winnipeg teams) and hops on the bus for the 20-minute trip to the MTS Centre. During the quiet ride, the only words that rise above the din of the engine are "Hi, Gabe," as a new passenger boards and an enthusiastic "Hi!" in response. He passes the media entrance more than an hour before the opening faceoff, but there's no need to flash his credentials, which he proudly wears around his neck. He makes his way into the main concourse, buys a large popcorn and bottle of water and sits in the stands for the pre-game videos and warmup.

And when the puck drops, it's go time. Langlois glides from section to section and puts on his moves during the musical interludes between play. Some involve an air guitar, some a 360-degree turn and others a fist-pump in the air. When he appears in a section, kids of all ages clap along, glad that Dancing Gabe has finally made it to their part of the building. When the music stops, he sits down in a nearby seat, if he can find one in the perpetually sold-out MTS Centre, or grabs his water bottle and scurries for the lobby to run around to the next section. When the music starts again, so does he.

And just like the coach's favorite player who gives his all regardless of the score, Langlois is no fairweather fan. He dances and cheers just as enthusiastically during wins and losses. Between periods, he gets the rockstar treatment, constantly slapping the open palms held out in front of him in the main concourse, as well as signing autographs and posing for pictures.

But Langlois isn't without controversy. A handful of fans resent the preferential treatment he gets, such as free admission to all pro games in Winnipeg. Whenever hecklers voice their displeasure, however, they're quickly drowned out by his fans.

"HE'S BEEN A LOYAL SUPPORTER OF THE JETS BRAND. WE'RE SUPPORTIVE OF PEOPLE WHO HAVE SUPPORTED US"

Langlois was even a hot topic of conversation when the Jets sold out their building (for three to five years, depending on the section) in a matter of minutes in June 2011. In the old Winnipeg Arena, there was rarely any concern about him finding a seat if he needed one. But would the reborn Jets let him in? Would there be a capacity issue? Did the team figure it had maintained enough ties to the past already? The controversy was short-lived, as True North Sports & Entertainment quickly confirmed that Langlois would be given a season's pass. Jets spokesman Scott Brown said the team wasn't going to leave him "out in the cold."

"He's been a loyal supporter of the Jets brand," Brown said. "We're supportive of people who have supported us."

GABE LANGLOIS

THE CONTENDERS

GREEN MEN

You probably don't know their names, but you know their outfits. Vancouver's Green Men, 'Force' (Adam Forsyth) and 'Sully' (Ryan Sullivan), are often seen in the two seats adjacent to the visitor's penalty box, clad in bright green, form-fitting body suits. The inspiration for their suits came from an episode of *It's Always Sunny in Philadelphia* in which a character wore a similar outfit.

When a Canucks opponent is sent there, they spring into action with all kinds of body movements, including handstands against the glass, and they often use props, such as a cardboard cut-out of actor Vince Vaughn (a noted Chicago Blackhawks fan) wearing a Canucks jersey and signs like "Legalize SJ Shark Fin Soup." It's all designed, of course, to be as big a distraction to the opposing players as possible. Over the past four seasons, some players have glanced over and had a laugh, but most ignore them. The NHL has noticed them, though, and has reportedly stepped in and asked the duo to tone down their antics. Forsythe and Sullivan were inducted into the ESPN Hall of Fans in 2012.

KEN CRUISE

Cruise has taken hockey fashion to a never-before-seen level. The 21-year-old Boston Bruins fan stitched together a business suit made entirely from the team's black and yellow rally towels. He collected his material during the 2011 playoffs while walking through TD Garden after a game. He picked up as many clean ones as he could and even a few that smelled of beer. The finished product comprises 27 towels, including a necktie signed by Bruins legend Derek Sanderson.

SHAWN CHAULK

There are fans, there are super-fans and then there's Chaulk, a construction contractor from Fort McMurray, Alta., who started buying game-used gear nearly 20 years ago to feel connected to the game he loved. Eventually, he amassed the greatest collection of Wayne Gretzky memorabilia ever assembled.

He sold off some prized possessions at an auction in June 2013, netting more than $500,000 for jerseys, skates, helmets, gloves and pucks used by No. 99. The jersey Gretzky wore in 1986-87, during which he scored his 500th NHL goal, fetched $350,000 alone.

Chaulk didn't sell everything, though. He kept a stick from The Great One's eight-game stint with the World Hockey Association's Indianapolis Racers (on which the equipment manager stamped "Gretsky") and the jersey from 1981-82 in which Gretzky shattered Phil Esposito's single-season scoring record with 92 goals.

CHAPTER 11

BIGGEST BLOCKBUSTER

THE WAYNE GRETZKY TRADE

BY ADAM PROTEAU

THERE HAVE BEEN THOUSANDS of trades made in NHL history, but when it comes to the biggest, most consequential, shocking and game-changing deal of all-time, there's no contest as to which one gets the nod: Wayne Gretzky from Edmonton to Los Angeles. The full exchange of talent was Gretzky, Marty McSorley and Mike Krushelnyski to the Kings and Jimmy Carson, Martin Gelinas, $15 million and three first-round picks to the Oilers. A simple list of the components, however, doesn't do justice to the true impact of the move.

The Gretzky trade didn't just resonate throughout the hockey world. It thundered across the entire sports landscape. Never before had a superstar of the highest caliber been dealt at the peak of his powers and in the immediate wake of winning a championship. Yet here was No. 99, just 27 years old and coming off his fourth Stanley Cup after a 149-point season, headed to a team that hadn't made it out of the first round of the playoffs in six years. And perhaps most importantly, the trade shook all of Canada, after losing a national and cultural icon to another country.

That's what happened when Gretzky changed NHL teams for the first time on Aug. 9, 1988, also known as the day all other NHLers realized it didn't matter how well they played, because even the best of them could be uprooted at any moment. It was the first trade that included a sufficiently enormous amount of money to do so and indicated how much of a big business professional hockey's highest level had become. And in the eyes of many, it set the stage for league expansion across the Sunbelt and the growth of the sport in non-traditional markets. But if you ask the centerpiece of the trade about it, he will tell you the people involved were focused only on the results they could control on the ice.

> **"WHEN I WAS DEALT TO L.A., MY ONLY MINDSET WAS I TRULY ENJOYED BEING ON A GOOD TEAM AND TRULY LOVED WINNING CHAMPIONSHIPS"**

"A lot of people still talk about me coming to Los Angeles to help hockey grow in California and the United States, but that really wasn't the case at all," Gretzky said. "When I was dealt to L.A., my only mindset was I truly enjoyed being on a good team and truly loved winning championships. I really never thought about growing the game or trying to make hockey bigger in L.A. I thought that would all come with the success of the organization and winning as a team."

Gretzky has no regrets about the trade and loved Los Angeles enough to raise his family there. He admitted, however, that he does sometimes think of what he and an intact Oilers dynasty team comprising multiple future Hall of Famers might have achieved.

"Could we have won seven, eight, nine championships? I don't know," Gretzky said. "Sometimes I think, 'Wow, it might have been fun.' But you never know what turns life is going to take."

WAYNE GRETZKY

THE CONTENDERS

MONTREAL CANADIENS TRADE PATRICK ROY AND MIKE KEANE TO THE COLORADO AVALANCHE FOR JOCELYN THIBAULT, MARTIN RUCINSKY AND ANDREI KOVALENKO

On Dec. 6, 1995, Canadiens coach Mario Tremblay effectively severed the team's ties with its star goalie after leaving Roy in net for nine goals in a period and a half at home against the Detroit Red Wings. Roy demanded a trade and was suspended before the team dealt him to the Avalanche four days after the game. He went on to win two more Cups, while Montreal fans were left bitter over what might have been were it not for a regrettable coaching move.

CHICAGO BLACK HAWKS TRADE PHIL ESPOSITO, KEN HODGE AND FRED STANFIELD TO THE BOSTON BRUINS FOR GILLES MAROTTE, PIT MARTIN AND JACK NORRIS

In May 1967, the Black Hawks had Stan Mikita and Bobby Hull as their top two offensive threats and felt they didn't need the 25-year-old Esposito, especially when the Bruins dangled physical blueliner Marotte on the trade market. Unfortunately for Chicago, Marotte never blossomed into a star. Esposito, Hodge and Stanfield, however, all played key roles in Boston's two Cups in the early 1970s, making this deal one of the most lopsided in league history.

EDMONTON OILERS TRADE MARK MESSIER AND FUTURE CONSIDERATIONS (JEFF BEUKEBOOM) TO THE NEW YORK RANGERS FOR BERNIE NICHOLLS, STEVEN RICE, LOUIE DEBRUSK AND FUTURE CONSIDERATIONS (DAVID SHAW)

Messier departed the Oilers three years after Gretzky did when he was dealt to Manhattan in October 1991 for a package that included veteran star Nicholls, top prospect Rice and enforcer DeBrusk. That DeBrusk was the one who lasted longest in an Oilers uniform, while Messier delivered the Rangers' first Stanley Cup in 54 years, shows how poorly the deal turned out for Edmonton. Heck, even the future considerations part of the trade benefitted the Blueshirts.

CHAPTER 12

BIGGEST TRADE

CALGARY–TORONTO 10-PLAYER DEAL

BY AARON PORTZLINE

WITH A CHUCKLE, VETERAN NHL executive Cliff Fletcher recalled the ironic aspect of his role in the biggest NHL trade – in sheer volume of players and picks (and cash) – ever consummated.

"Usually, there's a little apprehension regarding the players you're acquiring," Fletcher said. "But in this case, I knew the guys I was getting better than the guys I was trading. So, yes, it seemed like a pretty crazy deal in terms of scope… but I knew what I was doing."

Fletcher had been GM of the Atlanta/Calgary Flames for 19 years before leaving after 1990-91 to take over the Toronto Maple Leafs. After only six months on the job, Fletcher sprung a 10-player trade with his former team and his replacement, Flames GM Doug Risebrough. Toronto acquired Doug Gilmour, Jamie Macoun, Rick Wamsley, Ric Nattress and Kent Manderville from Calgary in exchange for Gary Leeman, Michel Petit, Jeff Reese, Craig Berube and Alexander Godynyuk on Jan. 2, 1992.

"We'd been talking about it since September," said Fletcher, now a special advisor for the Maple Leafs. "It was all over the map, a 1-for-1, 2-for-2, a 4-for-4, probably a 3-for-3 at some point… and then, ultimately, a 5-for-5."

By the sound of it, Fletcher would have gone 8-for-8 if Risebrough would have been willing.

"We had a really poor club right then – we were 10-25-5 at the halfway point – and I really wanted to make some changes," Fletcher said. "I felt like if we could just get Doug Gilmour into Toronto, we could start to get it turned around and so we started talking about Gilmour – there were some contractual issues between him and Calgary – and it just grew and grew."

The league doesn't keep such records, but it's believed to be the largest number of active players changing teams in one trade.

"I got a call from (Risebrough) when I was riding the bike after practice on New Year's Day," Wamsley said. "All he would tell me is that I was traded, not the entirety of the deal. Well, I started hearing from writers around the country and they knew the deal. They started saying the names and I just went, 'Whoa. Whoa! Wow!' "

DOUG GILMOUR

Because of Gilmour, the Leafs clearly won the deal. He set a franchise record with 127 points in 1992-93, followed it up with 111 points in 1993-94 and led Toronto to the conference final in both seasons. He was more than a point-per-game player in his six seasons with the Leafs.

"It turned everything around," Wamsley said. "We had 10 wins at the time of the trade and we almost made the playoffs that year."

The centerpiece from the Flames' perspective was expected to be Leeman, who had 113 goals during a three-year stretch as a right winger with Toronto in the late 1980s. Leeman was a flop in Calgary, though, scoring just 11 goals in 59 games. He was gone two seasons later. Nearly every other player in the deal for both clubs moved on to another team or retired within four years, most of them within two seasons.

It wasn't the biggest trade in North American sports history – in 1954, MLB's New York Yankees and Baltimore Orioles pulled off an 18-player trade – but it's the kind of swap that isn't likely in today's salary-capped NHL.

THE CONTENDERS

PHILADELPHIA FLYERS TRADE PETER FORSBERG, RON HEXTALL, CHRIS SIMON, MIKE RICCI, KERRY HUFFMAN, STEVE DUCHESNE, TWO FIRST-ROUND PICKS AND $15 MILLION TO THE QUEBEC NORDIQUES FOR ERIC LINDROS

Lindros' arrival in the NHL was a mess, from his yearlong holdout after Quebec drafted him No. 1 overall in 1991 to his eventual trade a year later, which required an arbitrator to decide. Ultimately, the Flyers won the right to trade for Lindros on June 30, 1992, but the Nordiques – and eventually the Colorado Avalanche – were the real winners. The Avalanche went on to win two Stanley Cups and eight consecutive division titles between 1995-96 and 2002-03, giving the franchise an NHL record of nine, including the Nordiques' final season.

NEW YORK ISLANDERS TRADE PAT LAFONTAINE, RANDY HILLIER, RANDY WOOD AND A FOURTH-ROUND PICK TO THE BUFFALO SABRES FOR PIERRE TURGEON, UWE KRUPP, BENOIT HOGUE AND DAVE MCLLWAIN

On the topic of holdouts, superstar LaFontaine refused to start 1991-92 as a member of the Islanders. With his hands tied, GM Bill Torrey shipped the 1983 third-overall pick to the Sabres eight games into the season. LaFontaine flourished, notching 148 points the following year, but after that he couldn't stay healthy. The Islanders got fair value, though, as first-overall pick (1987) Pierre Turgeon had some of his best seasons on Long Island. Krupp and Hogue proved solid additions as well.

TORONTO MAPLE LEAFS TRADE WENDEL CLARK, SYLVAIN LEFEBVRE, LANDON WILSON AND A FIRST-ROUND PICK TO THE QUEBEC NORDIQUES FOR MATS SUNDIN, GARTH BUTCHER, TODD WARRINER AND A FIRST-ROUND PICK

This deal from the 1994 off-season saw the Maple Leafs move Clark, their captain and one of the franchise's most beloved players, in a six-player swap, including a future Leafs captain and beloved player, namely Sundin. Of those six, Lefebvre was the only one to hoist the Stanley Cup, doing so with Colorado in 1996. Clark would eventually return to the Blue and White for two-plus seasons in 1996 and one last time in 2000 before retiring.

CHAPTER 13

BIGGEST BENCH BRAWL

MINNESOTA NORTH STARS vs. BOSTON BRUINS

BY RYAN KENNEDY

IT WAS AS OMINOUS a warning as an NHL official could get. Gord Broseker was skating around in warmups, ready to work a North Stars-Bruins game at the old Boston Garden with fellow linesman Kevin Collins and referee Dave Newell, when Minnesota right winger Tom Younghans skated by.

"I hope you and Kevin went to the gym today."

It was Feb. 26, 1981, and the two teams would soon make NHL history by brawling their way to 67 penalties after the first period – still an NHL record – and 84 in total, including 16 majors and 13 game misconducts.

"Back then, you had to put another player in the box if a guy got a misconduct," Broseker said. "We went over to the coaches and said we couldn't put all those guys in the box because we won't have any players. This is the rule, but we're going to waive it or else we'll have to cancel the game."

Glen Sonmor was the bench boss for Minnesota that night and if anyone deserves blame for the melee-filled evening, it's probably him. To this day, however, his North Stars charges still give him credit for inspiring them to stick up for each other against the big bad Bruins.

"It looked like we were going to match up with them in the first round of the play-offs," Younghans said. "And I remember at the team meal, while we were having dessert,

"I DON'T KNOW IF I WAS MORE SCARED ON THE ICE OR UP IN THE STANDING-ROOM ONLY SECTION IN MY SUIT AND TIE. THANK GOD NOBODY ATTACKED US UP THERE"

DINO CICCARELLI

GLEN SONMOR

Sonmor addressed us all. He started matching guys up: Jack Carlson and Stan Jonathan, Bobby Smith and Steve Kasper… He told us we were just as tough, but they play together. He emphasized how important it was to react. If someone breathed on you or looked at you cross-eyed, it was important to set the stage."

And set the stage they did. Seven seconds into the game, one of Sonmor's pairings found each other, with Smith (a player so accomplished the Ontario League hands out an academic award in his name) taking on the 5-foot-8 Kasper.

That was just the tip of the iceberg. After a couple more scraps, a line brawl erupted at the nine-minute mark and the archaic design of Boston Garden took center stage. The problem was that the hallway to the visitors' dressing room came right off Boston's bench, so any North Star kicked out of the game had to walk right by the entire Bruins team. Before long, the hallway was packed with brawling players, fans, security officials and even a cameraman who got stuck in the middle of the fray.

"The Bruins were standing up for their fans and the benches just emptied," Younghans said. "And when you're in a bench-clearing brawl, you don't know where that next punch is coming from."

Broseker doesn't even remember the hallway scrum because he had bigger problems on his hands. Specifically, a pair of 200-pounders named Craig Hartsburg and Brad McCrimmon. Minnesota's Hartsburg had just pounded on future Vancouver Canucks GM Mike Gillis, while McCrimmon fought a pair of North Stars. Broseker was hauling Hartsburg down the hallway to the visitors' dressing room when he saw McCrimmon running down the concrete, still in his skates. Thinking on his feet, Broseker yelled out to an old attendant in charge of the officials' dressing room.

"I yelled out, 'Herbie, open the door!' and I threw Hartsburg in," Broseker said. "Later, once I was back on the ice I thought, 'Geez, I wonder what happened to Hartsburg. He's probably tearing our room apart.' "

Broseker later found out that the accomplished defenseman had calmed down, so his clothes were safe. But the linesman also had to escort Sonmor past the Bruins to the bowels of the arena once the North Stars' coach was kicked out.

"That was a dandy," Broseker said. "He did not want to go."

Younghans was also tossed from the game and for him and several teammates it was

"IF IT HAPPENED TODAY, IT WOULD GO DOWN AS ONE OF THE FILTHIEST, DIRTIEST GAMES EVER"

truly a pick-your-poison scenario, since they spent the rest of the game up with the bleacher creatures.

"I don't know if I was more scared on the ice or up in the standing-room only section in my suit and tie," he said. "Thank God nobody attacked us up there."

Since the team's birth in 1967, the North Stars had never won a game at Boston Garden and on this night, nearly a decade and half later, the streak continued as the Bruins won what Broseker and his mates dubbed 'The Boston Massacre' by a score of 5-1. After the game, though, the North Stars weren't broken. Bloodied, sure, but they held their heads high knowing they had stood together. A few weeks later the teams did indeed meet in the playoffs and Minnesota swept the series.

"We lost that game, but we really did something about winning the war," Younghans said. "We were having a good season and that gave us an extra push."

As for Broseker, it was the second-most infamous game of his career – he also worked the Don Koharski-Jim Schoenfeld "Donut" incident – and one that dragged on into the wee hours of the night. Back then, officials had to file written reports on the evening's events and there was a lot to cover in a game that had so many penalties and ejections. Luckily, a couple more officials happened to be in the stands that night. John McCauley was in town getting treated for an eye injury at Massachusetts General Hospital while Terry Gregson was on a training assignment. Still, it was a lot of paperwork.

"It was two or three in the morning before I went to bed," Broseker said. "I'm not saying I didn't have a couple beers while I wrote those reports, but I definitely had a couple after."

Now retired, Broseker looks back at that game as part of a bygone era.

"If it happened today, it would go down as one of the filthiest, dirtiest games ever," he said. "Back then, those kinds of brawls were just part of the sport."

THE CONTENDERS

PUNCH-UP IN PIESTANY

The 1987 World Junior Championship lives on in infamy thanks to a bench-clearing brawl between Canada and the Soviet Union that got so out of control officials cut the lights in the arena. Brendan Shanahan, Sergei Fedorov and Theo Fleury were all part of the game, which ended with both teams disqualified. Canada had been in line to win gold.

THE GOOD FRIDAY BRAWL

Blood rivals Montreal and Quebec lived up to their billing when hostilities broke out on April 20, 1984. The Canadiens and Nordiques often brawled, but this bench-clearing melee featured the rare familial tilt of brothers Dale and Mark Hunter fighting each other. They now own and run the OHL's London Knights.

OTTAWA SENATORS VS. PHILADELPHIA FLYERS

The record-setter for most penalty minutes by both teams in one game (419), the Senators-Flyers tilt on March 5, 2004, featured oddities such as a goalie fight between Patrick Lalime and Robert Esche, Mark Recchi taking on Bryan Smolinski and Jason Spezza fighting Patrick Sharp.

CHAPTER 14

BIGGEST CHEAP SHOT

DALE HUNTER

BY WAYNE FISH

THERE'S AN UNWRITTEN, UNSPOKEN code in pro hockey that loosely says you don't go after the other team's skill players, especially not during the playoffs and certainly not in the middle of a goal celebration. That's why Dale Hunter's heinous hit on Pierre Turgeon in the first round of the 1993 playoffs stands atop the podium of all-time cheap shots.

One could make a case for the egregious acts of players such as Todd Bertuzzi or Marty McSorley, but those involved revenge for what the attackers perceived as wrong-doing. What Hunter, playing for the Washington Capitals, did to Turgeon, the offensive star of the New York Islanders, in Game 6 goes against the silent agreement of mutual respect generally found on NHL ice. Turgeon had just scored a late insurance marker to essentially wrap up the series when, during his joyous moment, Hunter came from nowhere and delivered a very late hit that separated Turgeon's shoulder and knocked him out of the first six games of the next round. For that cheap shot, Hunter received a 21-game suspension.

Twenty years later, Turgeon holds no grudge. His injuries didn't jeopardize his career, which he concluded in 2007 after a 19-year tenure. And he understands that Hunter, from whom Turgeon had stolen a pass to score the goal, was just acting out of frustration. To his credit, Hunter later expressed remorse and said he "would take it back if I could." But on the night of April 30, 1993, at Nassau Coliseum, emotions were running high.

"Obviously, at the time, you looked at it as a dirty play," said Turgeon's teammate at the time, Derek King, now an assistant coach with the American League's Toronto Marlies. "Over the years, you could look at it and see how Hunter could be frustrated by us beating them in that series. Hunter was a hard-nosed player. I don't want to say he was a dirty player, but he made it tough on you to play. But if he (Turgeon) can forgive him, I guess the rest of us ('93 Islanders) can, too."

Some believe that Hunter, the only NHL player ever to amass more than 1,000 points (1,020) and 3,000 penalty minutes (3,565), is a worthy candidate for the Hall of Fame. The Turgeon hit, however, might stick in the craw of some of the voters.

"He played both sides of the puck, played a tough game and did all the dirty work for

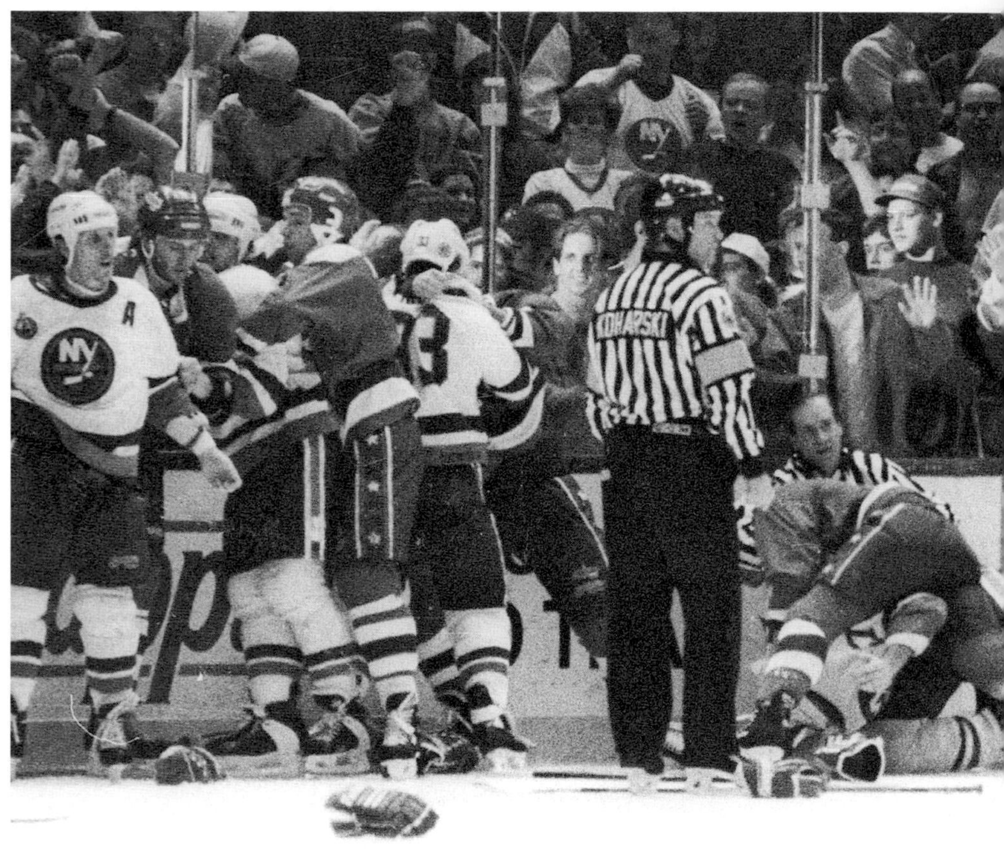

the team," said Craig Berube, Hunter's former Capitals teammate and a good friend. "I believe they (the Hall of Fame selection committee) look at different things when they vote. All I know is, he's the toughest guy who put points on the board that I've ever seen."

The ironic thing about the Turgeon hit is that Hunter never made a habit of going after guys who couldn't defend themselves. He wasn't the biggest energy guy (5-foot-10, 200 pounds), but he was willing to take on the big boys. And Hunter never came across as a typical cement-head. Just ask the Philadelphia Flyers, who had their Stanley Cup hopes dashed in 1988 when Hunter scored a breakaway goal in overtime of Game 7 in the opening round to send them home early.

Hunter has gone on to become a fine junior coach with the Ontario League's London Knights and even experienced some success at the NHL level when he came in as an interim coach with Washington in 2011. For one night in '93, however, he let frustration get the best of him and some people define his career by that one moment of indiscretion.

DALE HUNTER

"At the time, we were all pissed off at him," King said. "You wanted to club him over the head or try to get him. We shook it off. We knew we had a tough series ahead of us against Pittsburgh (and didn't want to risk suspensions)."

The honor code is there, but sometimes feelings can get out of control. It was just an unfortunate situation in an intense time of the season. And the threat of suspensions isn't necessarily an effective deterrent. Since the Hunter-Turgeon incident, several others have drawn longer suspensions, including ones instigated by Chris Simon, Jesse Boulerice and McSorley.

"I don't think he was trying to hurt Turgeon or separate his shoulder," King said. "I like to think that most guys don't try to put a guy out... There's just sportsmanship in the game. The Turgeon goal made it 5-3 and that's the last game of the series. To do (what Hunter did) when you have no chance of winning, at that time, it was tough for us to take."

BIGGEST CHEAP SHOT

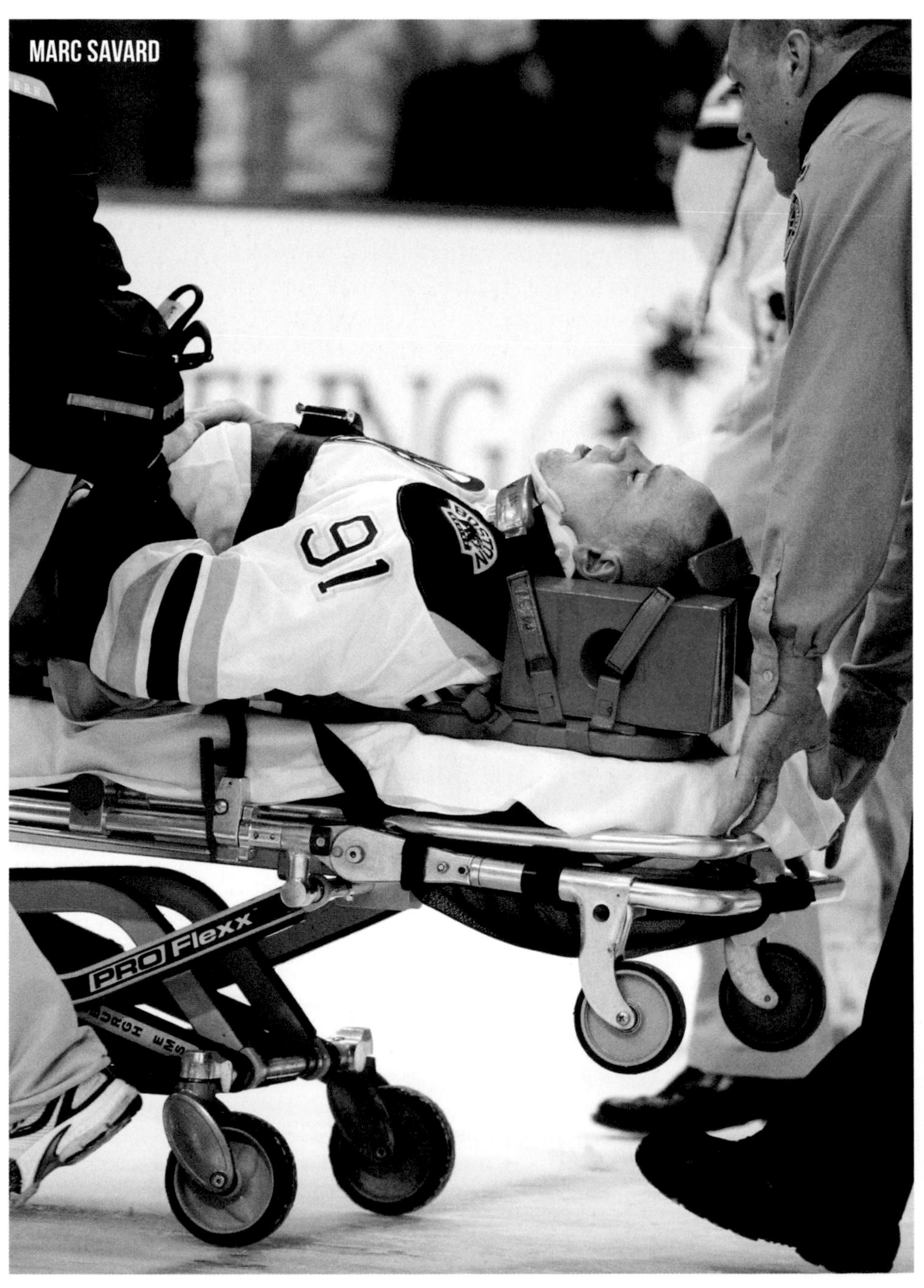

MARC SAVARD

THE CONTENDERS

TODD BERTUZZI AMBUSHES STEVE MOORE

Hockey grudges are notorious for ending in violence and this might be the all-time worst. On March 8, 2004, in a game between the Vancouver Canucks and Colorado Avalanche, Bertuzzi chased down Moore from behind to avenge Moore's hit on Canucks superstar Markus Naslund in a game three weeks earlier. The sucker punch and subsequent impact of Bertuzzi's weight landing on Moore's already unconscious body caused three broken vertebrae in Moore's neck, ending his career. Bertuzzi received a 20-game suspension.

MARTY MCSORLEY CLUBS DONALD BRASHEAR

Brashear had bashed McSorley in a battle of enforcers in the first period of a game between Boston and Vancouver on Feb. 20, 2000. Upset at being turned down for a rematch, McSorley, in the dying seconds of the game, swung his stick high and hit the Canucks tough guy in the head, causing a severe concussion. He said he didn't mean to injure Brashear, but the NHL turned a deaf ear to the apology, suspending the Bruins goon for a full calendar year (which amounted to 23 games). McSorley never played in the NHL again.

MATT COOKE BLINDSIDES MARC SAVARD

On March 7, 2010, Cooke connected shoulder to head as Savard cut into the middle of the ice, spinning the Bruins center around in a whirl of limbs and stick. Savard never saw him coming and had to be carried off on a stretcher. Cooke, then with the Pittsburgh Penguins, had a history of questionable on-ice actions, but received no suspension because the league hadn't yet taken steps to ban headshots. Technically, as then-NHL VP Colin Campbell put it afterward, the hit was within the rules. Savard returned in the playoffs and played 25 games in 2010-11, but never fully recovered. He didn't play at all in the next two seasons and his career is believed to be over because of Cooke's hit.

CHAPTER 15

BIGGEST SUSPENSION

BILLY COUTU

BY KYLE CICERELLA

RARELY DOES A HOCKEY player act so savagely that his actions get him banned for life. But 86 years ago, Boston Bruins defenseman Billy Coutu crossed the line and to this day he's still the only player ever to be handed a lifetime suspension by the NHL for a game-related incident.

Coutu, a hard-nosed, brutal player, entered the NHL in its inaugural season of 1917 with the Montreal Canadiens. He was a 5-foot-11, 190-pound bull who always tested the league's tolerance of how much violence would be accepted in the game.

"He was a pretty decent little player, but he hardly had a clean rap sheet," said hockey historian Greg Oliver. "He reminds me a little bit of a Chris Simon, someone who could play but got himself in trouble a little bit, too."

Coutu had already been part of some of hockey's most violent incidents when, in 1927, NHL president Frank Calder decided he'd seen enough from the defenseman, expelling the 35-year-old from the league for life for attacking referees Jerry Laflamme and Billy Bell.

"A firm example had to be laid," Oliver said. "It's so incredibly rare for lifetime bans to happen that he was definitely made an example of, whether that's right or wrong or not. It's one thing to semi-accidentally knock a ref down, but he attacked."

It was April 13, 1927, and the Ottawa Senators had defeated Boston 3-1 on home ice to win the Stanley Cup. The series went four games and both clubs had reasons to be upset with the refereeing. The Bruins, however, were already enraged with Laflamme before the final game had even started. Some players on the team, as well as GM Art Ross, believed Laflamme had it in for their club from the previous season. So after Ottawa was awarded a five-minute power play in the second period of Game 4, which led to the Senators taking a 2-0 lead, frustration boiled over.

"It's obvious the whole team had a hate-on for the guy," Oliver said.

Both clubs were out of control in the third period, with some players swinging their stick or butt-ending an opponent. By the time the final horn had sounded, the Bruins were enraged. Some reports originally said Coutu attacked Laflamme on the ice, but that's not the case.

BIGGEST SUSPENSION

BILLY COUTU

"He struck the referee," Oliver said, "but it was behind the scenes."

Boston had actually left the ice and returned to its dressing room, where it's believed Ross offered a $500 bonus to the first player to go find Laflamme.

"Art Ross definitely had a vendetta of sorts against referee Jerry Laflamme," Oliver said. "There were quotes afterwards (from teammate Frank Frederickson) that said Ross did offer the money."

Coutu left the Bruins' room after Ross' alleged offer and found Laflamme in a corridor of the Ottawa Auditorium. He knocked him to the ground with a punch and continued to assault him. When Bell tried to help his partner, Coutu tackled him to the ground as well.

"A FIRM EXAMPLE HAD TO BE LAID. IT'S SO INCREDIBLY RARE FOR LIFETIME BANS TO HAPPEN THAT HE WAS DEFINITELY MADE AN EXAMPLE OF, WHETHER THAT'S RIGHT OR WRONG OR NOT. IT'S ONE THING TO SEMI-ACCIDENTALLY KNOCK A REF DOWN, BUT HE ATTACKED"

Fans and, according to some reports, other Bruins players took shots at Laflamme while he was vulnerable until the police pulled him to safety, but Coutu took the fall for starting the entire confrontation. Calder handed Coutu a lifetime ban from the NHL to go along with a $100 fine.

"The amazing thing about Coutu is that he ended up being a referee afterwards," Oliver said. "Not in the NHL, but it wasn't like he didn't understand hockey."

After his banishment, Coutu played four more seasons split between the Canadian-American Hockey League and American Hockey Association. His expulsion from the NHL was eventually overturned on March 12, 1932, but he never returned. It's believed Coutu received his bonus from Ross at the end-of-the-year team luncheon.

BIGGEST SUSPENSION

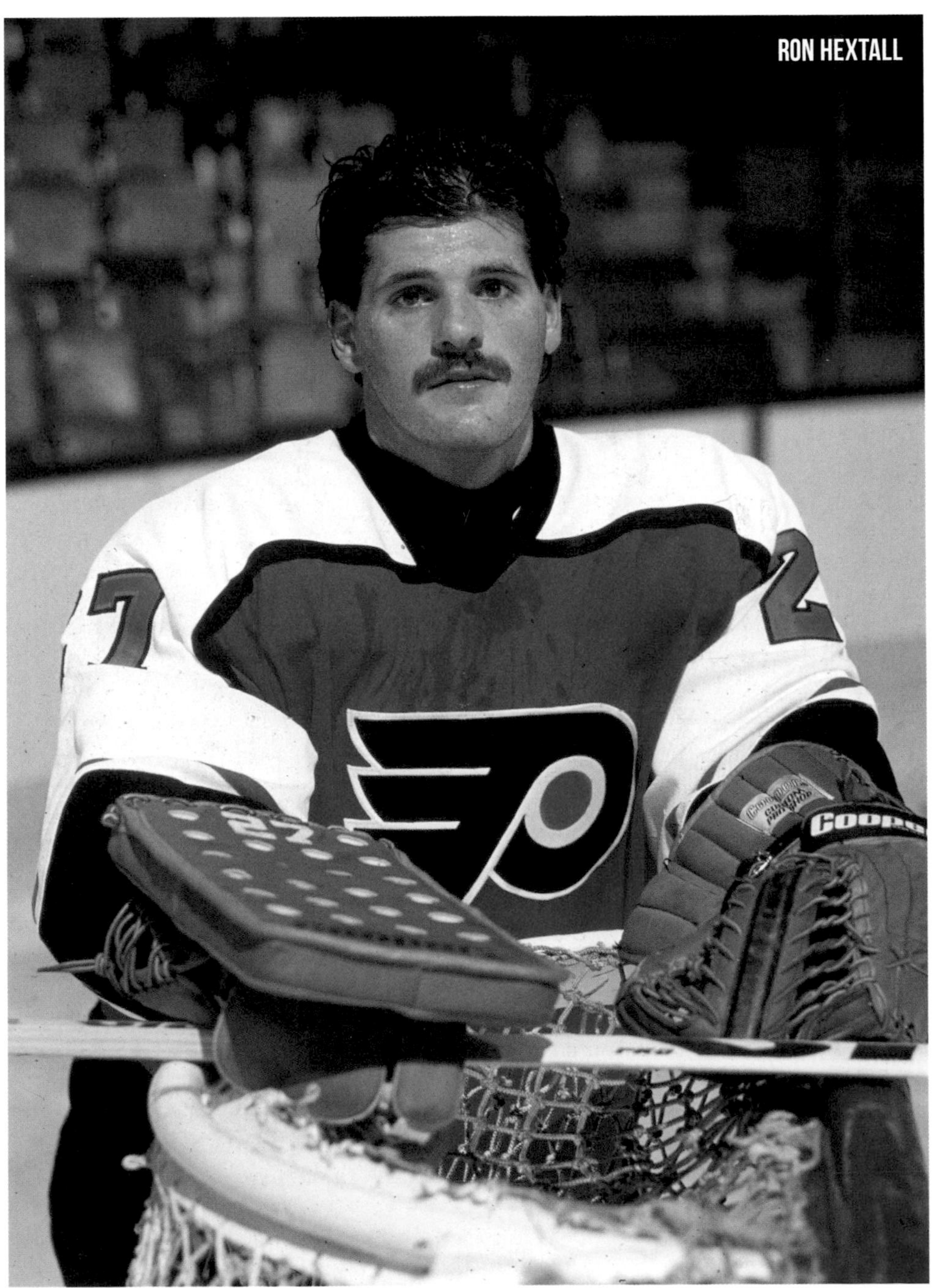

RON HEXTALL

THE CONTENDERS

CHRIS SIMON

Simon was suspended eight times in his 16-year career for everything from racial slurs to swinging sticks. While playing for the New York Islanders in December 2007, Simon knocked the Pittsburgh Penguins' Jarkko Ruutu to the ice during a stoppage of play and then violently stomped the Finn's right foot with his skate blade. There was no injury to Ruutu, but at the time of the incident Simon had only played 17 games since returning from a 25-game suspension for deliberately slashing the face of New York Ranger Ryan Hollweg in March 2007. The league gave Simon its biggest suspension of the modern era at 30 games.

RON HEXTALL

Fighting was a regular tactic for Hextall, who piled up more than 100 penalty minutes in a season for three years in a row in the late 1980s. But in May 1989 he earned the biggest suspension for a goaltender in NHL history after attacking the Montreal Canadiens' Chris Chelios in Game 6 of the Wales Conference final. With 1:37 to play, trailing by two and the season on the line, the one-time Vezina Trophy-winner made a beeline toward Chelios in the corner of the Philadelphia zone, attacking him and knocking him to the ice. A line brawl erupted and Hextall was given a match penalty for attempt to injure, which eventually led to a 12-game suspension.

ALEXANDER PEREZHOGIN

Perezhogin played 128 games for Montreal, but it's for his actions as a member of the American League's Hamilton Bulldogs that he may be best remembered. The Kazakhstan-born forward got tangled up with the Cleveland Barons' Garrett Stafford in front of the Barons' net in a playoff game on April 30, 2004. Stafford took a swing with his stick at Perezhogin after both players fell to the ice, but missed. Perezhogin retaliated with an axe chop to Stafford's face, which left him covered in blood and convulsing.

Stafford was given six games for his actions while Perezhogin was banned for the remainder of the post-season and all of the following year. In total, he missed 89 games.

CHAPTER 16

BIGGEST LINE

THE LEGION OF DOOM

BY GEOFF KIRBYSON

JOHN LECLAIR, ERIC LINDROS & MIKAEL RENBERG

GENERAL MANAGERS SCOUR THE Earth looking to get one player who's big, fast and offensively gifted. To find one is lucky. To get two on a team is a treasure. But three together on one line? Well, that just doesn't happen. Except for three seasons in the mid-1990s when the Philadelphia Flyers unleashed 'The Legion of Doom.'

The tale of the tape was staggering: Eric Lindros was 6-foot-4 and 230 pounds, John LeClair was 6-foot-3 and 226 pounds and Mikael Renberg was the shrimp at 6-foot-2 and 235 pounds.

BIGGEST LINE

It was the ultimate forward unit. The trio broke the mold of top lines in the NHL because all three players were almost as happy to beat their opponents in the corners as they were to best them on the scoreboard. There have been bigger threesomes thrown together, but none possessed a comparable combination of size, speed and skill.

Led by 'Big E,' the line terrorized the rest of the NHL for nearly three seasons, starting in 1994-95 after a lockout. LeClair arrived via a trade from the Montreal Canadiens and was slotted alongside Lindros and Renberg. The impact was immediate. Together, the three scored 80 goals and added 96 assists for 176 points in that shortened season. Lindros had 70 points in 46 games, winning the Hart Trophy and the Ted Lindsay Award. He and LeClair were named first-team all-stars, too.

It was during this time that teammate Jim Montgomery invented the nickname and the team's broadcaster, Gene Hart, popularized it. The next season was the line's most productive: they scored 121 goals and added 134 assists. During their third and final full season together, they scored 104 goals and had 131 assists.

The Flyers broke up The Legion of Doom during the 1997 off-season when they traded Renberg to the Tampa Bay Lightning. The line reunited briefly when Renberg returned to the Flyers midway through 1998-99, but he was dealt again the next season.

CLARK GILLIES, BRYAN TROTTIER & MIKE BOSSY

THE CONTENDERS

SESAME STREET LINE

One of The Legion of Doom's predecessors in Philadelphia was a line of Dave Schultz ('Grouch'), who was 6-foot-1 and 185 pounds, Orest Kindrachuk ('Ernie'), who was 5-foot-10 and 175 pounds, and Don Saleski ('Big Bird'), who was 6-foot-2 and 186 pounds. They were key cogs for the Broad Street Bullies in the early to mid-1970s and were the only NHL line named after Muppet characters. They played bigger than their actual size, in large part because of their ferocious checking and willingness to do anything – legal or otherwise – to win. (Schultz racked up a record 472 minutes in penalties in 1974-75. The 400-minute mark has only been broken three other times, including once more by Schultz.) All three members have a pair of Stanley Cup rings (1973-74 and 1974-75).

THE TRIO GRANDE

Literally 'The Big Three,' this line of the New York Islanders formed during Mike Bossy's rookie season in 1977-78. The six-foot, 185-pound right winger was matched up with Bryan Trottier (5-foot-11, 195 pounds) and Clark Gillies (6-foot-3, 210 pounds). Trottier was the playmaker and Bossy the sniper, while Gillies, who was best known for his physical play, showed excellent touch around the net, scoring 30 goals for four straight seasons. In addition to being all-stars, having their numbers retired and being elected to the Hall of Fame, 'The Trio Grande' also played a huge role in the Islanders' four-year Stanley Cup run from 1980 to 1983.

THE SMURF LINE

These three played big. They weren't going to beat you in the alleys, but they could beat you on the scoresheet. In the mid-1990s, the Canadiens sent the 5-foot-10, 165-pound Saku Koivu out between Valeri Bure (5-foot-11, 168 pounds) and Oleg Petrov (5-foot-9, 166 pounds) against opponents who dwarfed them. The diminutive trio used a different form of intimidation – speed and stickhandling skills – to slip past lead-footed defensemen.

CHAPTER 17

BIGGEST HITTER

SCOTT STEVENS

BY MICHAEL TRAIKOS

HELLO DARKNESS, MY OLD friend.

So goes the opening line of Simon & Garfunkel's 1964 folk classic, *The Sound of Silence*. With Scott Stevens on the ice, it was more like the sound of violence. His hits were beautiful, but nasty. Like watching full-contact gymnastics. Skating through the neutral zone as though he were an ornery bull, the hulking defenseman hit to hurt and was responsible for more yard sales than a Sunday morning in July.

Nobody was off-limits. Big or small, fourth-liner or all-star, Stevens didn't discriminate. His legendary open-ice hits on Eric Lindros and Paul Kariya defined each player's career. He once hit Ron Francis so hard the now-Hall of Fame center had to crawl back to the bench on his hands and knees.

Today, Stevens' victims would be permanently confined to a dark room and he would be a regular visitor to the NHL's disciplinary office for the number of concussions he caused. But back then he was romanticized as a sort of Dracula on skates. Feared, but also revered.

"He knew how to balance it out," said Ken Daneyko, who played 12 seasons with Stevens in New Jersey. "When he was younger, he took bad penalties, his timing wasn't always there and he got caught. But as he matured as a player, he knew when to step up when the team needed a lift and he perfected his timing. He was like a heat-seeking missile. He hung in the weeds and it's amazing that guys didn't see him."

When asked for some of his favorite Stevens hits, Daneyko mentioned the obvious ones:

"HE WAS LIKE A HEAT-SEEKING MISSILE. HE HUNG IN THE WEEDS AND IT'S AMAZING THAT GUYS DIDN'T SEE HIM"

BIGGEST HITTER

SCOTT STEVENS

the time he knocked the Detroit Red Wings' Slava Kozlov out of the second game of the 1995 Stanley Cup final and then barked to Dino Ciccarelli, "You're next!", the head-on collision with Lindros in Game 7 of the 2000 Eastern Conference final, and the 2001 playoff series against the Carolina Hurricanes when he practically blew up the entire roster.

"You don't see those anymore – it's a lost art," Daneyko said. "Now people think they're illegal, but very rarely did he leave his feet. But who cares? That was the time back then. His timing was terrific. Those big, open-ice hits are hard to do."

He paused and added, "Well, he got me great, too. I'm in his top 10 hits."

Daneyko is talking about the time he rushed the puck through the middle and got caught by a hipcheck from Stevens, who was with the Washington Capitals at the time. Daneyko tried to jump out of the way, but ended up cartwheeling through the air and landing on his head.

"I did a 360 pretty well," Daneyko said with a laugh. "He got me low and I went flying. The coaching staff, they showed that in practice one day early on when he came to New Jersey, for a good chuckle for the guys."

For Stevens' victims, laughing at their misfortune was really their only recourse. Well, they could retaliate. But Stevens, whose 2,785 penalty minutes are the second-most (behind Chris Chelios) of any player in the Hall of Fame, was likely going to damage them even more. That was the thing about the 6-foot-2, 215-pound defenseman. He could hurt the opposition in many ways. He once scored 21 goals in a season, led the Devils with 78 points in 1993-94 and finished his career with 908 points. But bodychecking was his calling card.

"It would be nice to be remembered as the greatest hitter in the game," Stevens once told The Hockey News. "That would be a great honor. To be able to do that for so many years is something I'm proud of, to be able to do it clean and to help my team."

Daneyko said life became easier when Stevens was on his side. But if any Devils teammate thought he could skate around the neutral zone without his head up, he had another thing coming.

"If we were in a slump, he'd make guys pay in practice," Daneyko said. "He wanted to give guys a wakeup call to let them know that he wasn't happy and that we needed to pay more attention to detail."

The way Stevens played, combined with the emergence of goaltender Martin Brodeur, allowed the Devils to build a team around a defense-first approach that resulted in three Stanley Cups. Stevens also changed. With Washington and the St. Louis Blues, he was known as a high-risk, high-reward player, who searched for big goals and big hits. In New Jersey, he developed into more of a shutdown role.

"He competed in every second of the day," said New Jersey GM Lou Lamoriello. "It was his leadership quality of not expecting anything less than the best. When he came here, he reduced his point production, not because he couldn't have done it, but because he was given a different role as far as being a shutdown guy. And he thrived on that, because winning, to Scott, was the most important thing, not statistics."

"IT WOULD BE NICE TO BE REMEMBERED AS THE GREATEST HITTER IN THE GAME. THAT WOULD BE A GREAT HONOR. TO BE ABLE TO DO THAT FOR SO MANY YEARS IS SOMETHING I'M PROUD OF, TO BE ABLE TO DO IT CLEAN AND TO HELP MY TEAM"

When asked if Stevens would be able to play the same way today, with the rule changes regarding hits to the head and the video reviews that freeze-frame every collision as though it were the Zapruder film, Lamoriello stopped to think before answering.

"Let me put it this way: would Scotty still be the same quality player? Yes," Lamoriello said. "Would he be allowed to do what he did? I couldn't answer that. Look at the media cry after every hit. I don't mean that in a critical way, but that's the era we're in. Concussions have come to the forefront and rightfully so. But there is no question in my mind that no one hit cleaner and better than Scotty. He was just a special player. Not only as a hitter, but in all aspects of the game."

THE CONTENDERS

NIKLAS KRONWALL

The Detroit defenseman has achieved such notoriety with his hits along the boards that "Kronwalled" is now in the hockey lexicon. All his bodychecks look the same: an opposing player exits the zone along the right side of the ice and Kronwall charges backward toward him, winding his legs like a pull-back car toy to generate maximum speed, before exploding on contact. The result, like the time he knocked out Martin Havlat in Game 3 of the 2009 Western Conference final against the Chicago Blackhawks, can be devastating.

WENDEL CLARK

The longtime Toronto Maple Leafs captain was only 5-foot-11 and weighed less than 200 pounds during his playing days, but few in the NHL played bigger. His hit on St. Louis Blues defenseman Bruce Bell as he was circling behind the net during a game in 1986-87 was like a sandcastle being levelled by a tidal wave. Bell left the game on a stretcher.

ZDENO CHARA

The so-called gentle giant has a mean side that comes out every now and then. When it does, watch out. Max Pacioretty fractured his neck and suffered a concussion after the 6-foot-9 Chara drove the Montreal Canadiens left winger WWE-style into the vertical stanchion at the end of the bench in 2011. That same season, former Maple Leafs center Mikhail Grabovski had "birds in his eyes" after Chara sandwiched him into the end boards. The lesson? Don't make the giant angry.

BIGGEST HITTER

WENDEL CLARK

CHAPTER 18

BIGGEST COACHING GAFFE

DON CHERRY

BY STAN FISCHLER

BY 1978-79, DON CHERRY wasn't the most successful NHL coach, but he was certainly the most popular. Featuring humor and outlandish comments, the Boston Bruins bench boss had a press persona that had climbed to the top of the hockey celebrity hit parade. 'Grapes' had become the toast of Beantown.

"Had I accomplished one more thing," Cherry said, "I might have become governor of Massachusetts."

That "thing" was no small matter, since he was alluding to the Stanley Cup, which happened to be mortgaged by the Montreal Canadiens for three consecutive years. And since the Habs had finished first that season with a 52-17-11 record to lead the league, all signs suggested another championship parade would be held in Montreal. Cherry's big bad Bruins, meanwhile, had topped the Adams Division (43-23-14) with Rick Middleton leading the attack and Brad Park anchoring the defense.

"My guys put in a good day's work," Cherry said, "and never bitched about it."

That lunch-pail athletic club philosophy paid off in the 1979 playoffs when Boston steamrolled the Pittsburgh Penguins in four straight first-round games to meet Montreal in the semifinal.

"We knew that if we could get past the Canadiens, we could win the Cup," Cherry said.

Montreal won the first two contests, but Boston rebounded and forced a Game 7 at the Forum on March 10, 1979. And the Bruins looked to have completed the comeback, leading the Canadiens 4-3 with fewer than four minutes remaining.

"We were looking at the biggest victory of our lives," Cherry said.

Then it happened.

As Montreal's Guy Lafleur skated off the ice, his shadow, Don Marcotte, did likewise for Boston. But there was a mix-up at the Bruins' bench. Suddenly, Marcotte shouted, "Oh, no!" Boston had too many men on the ice. Linesman John D'Amico noticed the Bruins had six skaters, but hesitated to blow his whistle. According to Cherry, D'Amico was waiting for one of his players to realize what had happened and make it back to the bench. Finally, however, his arm had to go up.

"I didn't have to count the players – I knew," Cherry said. "What I needed then was a

BIGGEST COACHING GAFFE

DON CHERRY

> **"I DIDN'T HAVE TO COUNT THE PLAYERS – I KNEW. WHAT I NEEDED THEN WAS A LARGE HOOK TO HAUL IN MY WANDERING MINSTREL"**

large hook to haul in my wandering minstrel. If the referee and linesmen wore blindfolds for about a minute, I might have been able to get somebody's attention and get him back to the bench before we were slapped with a two-minute penalty."

Once the whistle blew for the penalty, Cherry checked the Canadiens' bench.

"The Montreal players looked like a pride of lions about to jump a wildebeest," he said.

Boston was penalized and Lafleur then beat goalie Gilles Gilbert to force overtime. Yvon Lambert got the winner for the Canadiens at 9:33 of sudden death.

Who was at fault for the sixth skater gaffe? Cherry always tried to protect his players involved in ticklish situations and in this case he refused to name names, though it's generally believed the extra player was one of Cherry's favorites, Stan Jonathan. Cherry insisted the Bruins made a silent pact never to mention his name.

"The confusion was rooted in the fact that Marcotte has stayed on left wing through three shifts," Cherry said. "The other guy (Jonathan) was nervous and got carried away. When he finally came back to the bench after D'Amico had whistled the penalty, he had tears in his eyes. I wanted to cry myself, but I couldn't.

"I accepted full responsibility. It was the blunder of blunders. I deserved to be court-martialled."

THE CONTENDERS

JACK ADAMS

During the 1941-42 Stanley Cup final between Detroit and Toronto, the Red Wings led the series 3-0 and appeared ready to sweep the Maple Leafs in Game 4 at Olympia Stadium. Detroit's vitriolic coach, however, seethed as his club blew a two-goal, first-period lead and a one-goal lead in the third as Toronto rallied for a 4-3 win. Adams was so infuriated over the loss and officiating that he vaulted the boards at game's end, raced across the ice and proceeded to punch out referee Mel Harwood.

NHL president Frank Calder viewed the fracas and when the ice had cleared he imposed a Draconian punishment on Adams. Calder suspended the Motor City

JACK ADAMS

THE CONTENDERS

hockey boss indefinitely from the final. Adams' replacement was veteran Ebbie Goodfellow, who had never coached before. And it showed. The Leafs ran off 9-3, 3-0 and 3-1 victories to win the Cup. And all because of the crossed Adams' right cross to Harwood.

VIKTOR TIKHONOV

On the eve of the 1980 Winter Olympics, the U.S.S.R. was the prohibitive favorite to win gold in men's hockey. Everything about the Soviets, from coach Tikhonov to future Hall of Fame goalie Vladislav Tretiak, was first class and a 10-3 exhibition win over the United States underlined the point. Nor did anything the Redshirts do once the Games began change any minds about Soviet supremacy.

When the time came to play the U.S. in the semifinal, another rout by the Soviets was expected. Tikhonov's club led 2-1 late in the first period, but the Americans tied the game with one second remaining in the opening frame. Then came Tikhonov's shocking decision between periods to bench Tretiak and replace him with backup Vladimir Myshkin. Well into the third, Myshkin kept the Americans at bay by a 3-2 margin. Suddenly, Johnson scored again, followed by captain Mike Eruzione, and the game ended with the 'Miracle on Ice': Team USA won 4-3. As for Tikhonov, on further reflection, he admitted that pulling Tretiak was "the worst mistake of my coaching life."

ROBBIE FTOREK

New Jersey Devils coach Robbie Ftorek couldn't believe his eyes on Jan. 29, 2000, at Joe Louis Arena. His premier penalty killer, Jay Pandolfo, had been hit from behind by Detroit's Mathieu Dandenault and had plunged headfirst into the boards. Writhing in a growing pool of blood, Pandolfo eventually required 83 stitches to close his various wounds. Even more startling to Ftorek was referee Steve Walkom's decision not to call a penalty. When Kirk Maltby scored for the Red Wings on the ensuing counterattack, Ftorek went bananas. He grabbed a heavy wooden bench and tossed it on the ice. Walkom tossed Ftorek out of the game, but that wasn't the worst of it for the coach. New Jersey lost 3-1, he was suspended one game and fined $10,000 and the Devils lost nine of 16 games down the stretch.

Never one to approve of such antics, New Jersey GM Lou Lamoriello finally fired Ftorek fewer than two months later, despite the Devils still sitting in first place. His replacement, Larry Robinson, then calmly led New Jersey to its second Stanley Cup.

CHAPTER 19

BIGGEST FASHION FAUX PAS

JEAN-GUY TALBOT

BY BRIAN COSTELLO

JEAN-GUY TALBOT SHOULD HAVE known better.

He was living and working in the fashion mecca of North America. His office at Madison Square Garden was a few blocks from New York's garment district, just one mile down 7th Avenue from the fashion gurus at *Gentlemen's Quarterly*, and he had in his dressing room some of the game's coolest players of all-time: Ron Duguay, Phil Esposito and Dave Maloney. Those three, along with Anders Hedberg, even did television commercials for fashionable Sasson jeans.

Meanwhile, Talbot was creating the fashion violation of the century, at least in the hockey world. Take a glimpse at this photo of Talbot coaching the New York Rangers in 1977-78. Just look at him wearing a turtleneck sweater underneath a gaudy polyester tracksuit. You should know this photo wasn't taken during a practice or training camp session. It was taken during an actual game, one of 30 or 40 that season in which Talbot wore that hideous tracksuit. While the dapper likes of Don Cherry in Boston, Bob Pulford in Chicago, Scotty Bowman in Montreal and Al Arbour on Long Island dressed in tailor-made suits and custom-fitted Dack's, Talbot looked like he was heading out to mow the lawn on a brisk autumn morning.

Getting dressed wasn't always a white-flag event for Talbot. The 1977-78 season was an aberration. Talbot had a sterling 16-year career in which he won the Stanley Cup seven times, including in his first five years in the NHL, and lost in the final four other times. He wore a suit and tie before and after games, like his teammates Maurice Richard and Jean Beliveau in the early days and Gilbert Perreault and Garry Unger in his twilight seasons.

Talbot retired from playing in 1971 and moved straight into coaching with the Western League's Denver Spurs later that year. Like other bench bosses, he donned a suit and tie and made his way up the ranks to the NHL. He coached the St. Louis Blues in 1972-73 and 1973-74, but he wasn't crazy about the experience, so he returned to Denver in the minor leagues and World Hockey Association. When his former Canadiens teammate and Rangers GM John Ferguson called in the summer of 1977 asking him to coach in the Big Apple, Talbot accepted.

In the 1970s, tracksuits grew in popularity as athletes, especially Olympians seen on

BIGGEST FASHION FAUX PAS

JEAN-GUY TALBOT

television, wore them before and after competitions. "Aerobics" became a buzzword. The surge in synthetic fibers also took off that decade and Talbot got caught in a perfect storm of sweat, sweatpants and practical decision-making.

You see, Talbot was prone to perspiration. As a player, it was no big deal. But as a coach in a jam-packed arena with television lights and pressure and reporters and nerves and post-game conferences and questions... well, it made him sweat. Profusely.

"It gets hot in Madison Square Garden," Ferguson said in 1988. "You sweat a lot. If you're wearing a suit or sports jacket, it gets damp from the sweat. There are also puddles of water from the melting ice and that can ruin a suit."

It got to the point partway through 1977-78 where Talbot would take off his suit jacket after a game in the steamy quarters outside the dressing room and the sweat stains under his arms made it look like he had burned more calories than his players.

"I was embarrassed," said Talbot, 81. "I asked John (Ferguson), 'Will you let me wear a tracksuit during games? They're looser and more comfortable. After a game, I take a shower and it feels good to put on a clean, dry suit instead of one that's damp from the sweat.'

"I ASKED JOHN (FERGUSON), 'WILL YOU LET ME WEAR A TRACKSUIT DURING GAMES?' I THINK JOHN FELT BAD FOR ME SO HE DIDN'T ARGUE WITH IT"

"I think John felt bad for me so he didn't argue with it. He let me do it for the last half of the season."

An NHL coach wearing a tracksuit wasn't that huge of a deal in the loosey-goosey 1970s, a decade infused with disco lights and manmade Ultrasuede leisure suits. It was more of a footnote. With the passage of time, however, the "Aw, really?" factor gets ramped up.

It wasn't a good season for the Rangers. They struggled from the outset, Ferguson denied rumors in February that the team was considering a coaching change and later a first-round playoff loss sealed Talbot's fate. His coaching career was over. The tracksuit behind the bench died right then and there.

"I don't think you'll see anyone try that again," Talbot said.

That we can be sure of.

THE CONTENDERS

BARRY BECK

Beck was a bigger-than-life player after getting drafted second overall in 1977. Following two seasons with the Colorado Rockies, 'Bubba' was traded to the Rangers and before long New York was his. Named captain by the age of 23, Beck had the swagger and attitude to do things his own way, including strutting down the runway wearing this skimpy bathing suit and cowboy boots for a Manhattan fashion show in 1981.

MARC BERGEVIN

Seriousness aside, Canadiens GM Bergevin was a big jokester in his playing days. Some say the biggest in the game. The 2004-05 lockout shortened his career, but when coaching the Primus Worldstars in an exhibition game of NHLers against the Norwegian All-Stars in Oslo in 2004, he did get his team laughing when he dressed up in a toga to look like Caesar.

BERNIE NICHOLLS

Nicholls is an Ontario country boy at heart, but he enjoyed embracing the Los Angeles lifestyle when he played a decade for the Kings in the 1980s. He created the 'Pumper-Nicholl' windmill fist-pump after scoring a goal and took to softening his dirty blond hair a lighter color in the California sun. Nicholls was also seen from time to time wearing a full-length fur coat after games.

BARRY BECK

CHAPTER 20

BIGGEST FITNESS FREAK

ROD BRIND'AMOUR

BY MATT LARKIN

MARTIN GELINAS WENT THROUGH a lot in his 19-year NHL career. He was one of the pieces the Los Angeles Kings traded for Wayne Gretzky and later played in two Stanley Cup finals, winning once. His greatest challenge, however, may have been working out alongside Rod Brind'Amour.

One summer in the early 2000s, when the two were with the Carolina Hurricanes, team trainer Pete Friesen invited Gelinas to join Brind'Amour as he put him through a workout. On the agenda: running up and down the stairs at the then-RBC Center.

"I thought I was in pretty good shape, so I'm doing stairs, I'm getting on top of the stairs and I'm barely breathing," Gelinas said. "And then you've got Rod, doing the same thing with a 50-pound vest on him. That's the kind of guy he is."

The neat thing about Rod 'The Bod' Brind'Amour: he's been that kind of guy as long as he's played hockey. Sure, he was chiselled like a Greek god late in his career, winning both of his Frank Selke Trophies and his Cup after turning 35. But he isn't one of those players who coasted on raw talent in his teens and 20s before awakening to fitness. For Brind'Amour, it started early and, well, early. He was 12 years old and he was watching his dad rise day after day at 6:00 a.m. to work as a pipe fitter at a mill.

"He would get up and go and I remember him telling me, 'You don't want this job,'" Brind'Amour said with a laugh. "He said, 'You're going to have to do something different than any other kid to not be this. Every other kid sleeps in, every other kid's going to practice at the regular times. What are you going to do that separates you?'

"It sunk in for me: 'I better start lifting weights.'"

Brind'Amour didn't exactly ease himself into the lifestyle. He'd lift whenever his dad left for work in the morning and repeat the program after school. He was already a fitness fanatic, far ahead of his competition, when he played minor and junior hockey in his teen years and especially when he suited up for the Michigan State Spartans in college. As the urban legend goes, the Spartans' coaching staff had to lock Brind'Amour out of the gym some days so he would stop training so hard. Today, he confirms that the rumor, though exaggerated, is true. Michigan State always played Fridays and Saturdays at the time, with Sundays off. But he'd work out on Sundays, too.

ROD BRIND'AMOUR

"They just found a way for me to not be able to get into the building on those days," Brind'Amour said. "But it wasn't so much that (the workouts) were hurting me. They just thought I needed the rest. I understand that now, and obviously over the years – that you need rest as well. But when you're 18 years old and you want to get to the NHL, I figured I could rest later."

Brind'Amour remained a fitness fanatic during his NHL career and if it seemed he was in better shape every year, it's because he was. Brind'Amour never stopped adding to his routines. With Carolina, he'd get a manual of exercises from Friesen and would add his own on top of the program, whether it was extra lifting, stairs, skating or even Pilates. "I always had to be the hardest-working guy," Brind'Amour said. "Or at least no one was going to work harder. So I had no excuses when I hit the ice. It wasn't, 'Oh man, I didn't come in good enough shape.' "

Occasionally, he looks back and can't believe what he was capable of. On some days, he'd complete an "insane" track workout, then lift weights at the rink, then hit the ice. His philosophy: set the bar so high that you're ahead of the pack even if you fall short.

"ROD IS HIS OWN MAN. HE KEPT PUSHING HIMSELF. HE ALWAYS DID A LOT MORE THAN EVERYBODY ELSE AND THAT'S WHY HE'LL BE REMEMBERED AS THE LEGEND HE IS RIGHT NOW"

"We figured if we could do half of what he did, we would be in good shape," Gelinas said. "Rod is his own man. He kept pushing himself. He always did a lot more than everybody else and that's why he'll be remembered as the legend he is right now."

Now retired and an assistant coach with the Hurricanes, Brind'Amour's specialty is – surprise, surprise – conditioning. He believes kids and their teams make one key mistake today: not customizing their workouts. Teams often give the same program to every player when certain kinds – say, a bruising power forward versus a slick-skating offensive defenseman – require different types of physical attributes. Brind'Amour also believes that, though independent trainers can work wonders, players should consult with their team trainers first, as their own teams know them inside and out.

"We'll send a kid to whoever, but say, 'You've got to come back in better shape conditioning-wise. You've got to be able to go up and down the ice for 35 seconds and not tire out,' " Brind'Amour said. "'We don't need you to bench-press a car.' "

An ironic statement coming from someone more likely than any other NHL player to accomplish that feat.

BIGGEST FITNESS FREAK

CHRIS CHELIOS

THE CONTENDERS

GARY ROBERTS

Now retired, the former NHL power forward is regarded as *the* trainer for any player looking to take his fitness and overall game to new heights. Interestingly, he didn't become a workout monster until midway through his career. Chronic neck injuries knocked Roberts out for more than a year and he thought his playing days were done. He re-evaluated his diet and exercise regimen to fix his body, played 11 more seasons and became obsessed with training. Nowadays, if a player isn't pulling his weight, people say, "Just drop him off at Gary Roberts' doorstep and leave him there for the summer."

CHRIS CHELIOS

Anyone who plays in the NHL as a 48-year-old has to be in unbelievable shape, so it's no surprise to see Chelios crack this list. In the twilight of his career, his epically demanding workout regimen included exercises like biking at high speeds in a sauna as he and trainer T.R. Goodman made his body bulletproof, or resistant to any injury outside of freak occurrences. Chelios' physique allowed him to play with teammates 30 years his junior as an Atlanta Thrasher in his final season.

JAROMIR JAGR

No. 68 is living proof that finesse players don't have to be soft players. Jagr has dazzled with his puckhandling throughout his career, but part of why he protects the biscuit so well is his sculpted, immovable 240-pound frame. He turned himself into human granite through years of tireless, unorthodox training. His regular routines include taking to the ice at midnight to work on skills alone, practising while wearing a weight vest and strengthening his wrists by putting a barbell on the end of his stick blade.

CHAPTER 21

BIGGEST PAYROLL

2003-04 DETROIT RED WINGS

BY BOB DUFF

THE BEST HOCKEY TEAM cash could buy only served to prove the proverb money can't buy happiness.

After 2002-03, the Detroit Red Wings had a decision to make. They were loaded down with so many veteran players and lockout Armageddon was looming just around the corner as the NHL's collective bargaining agreement was set to expire on Sept. 15, 2004. A hard salary cap was likely in the league's future, so Detroit owner Mike Ilitch loaded up for 2003-04 and went for it one more time, even though that approach had proven a dismal failure one year earlier when, with a payroll of $68,410,500, the Red Wings were swept in the first round of the playoffs by the Anaheim Ducks and their payroll of some $45 million. It was the first time that had happened to a defending Stanley Cup champion since the Toronto Maple Leafs in 1951-52.

"Economics isn't going to prevent us from competing with the elite teams for the Stanley Cup," said Wings GM Ken Holland shortly after the abrupt end to the season.

As promised, Detroit anted up, signing unrestricted free agent defenseman Derian Hatcher for $6 million a season and bringing back retired goalie Dominik Hasek by picking up a $6-million option on his contract. Since they already had Curtis Joseph on the payroll for $8 million, it meant the Wings were paying out $14 million to their top two goalies alone. And Detroit had several other players with big contracts on the books: defensemen Nicklas Lidstrom ($10 million) and Chris Chelios ($5.9 million), and forwards Brendan Shanahan ($6.5 million), Steve Yzerman ($5.9 million) and Brett Hull ($5 million). To say the Wings were big spenders would be like saying Toronto fans find the Maple Leafs' 46-year Stanley Cup drought a bit of a nuisance.

It all amounted to an NHL-record payroll of $77,856,109. All that money, however, didn't add up to success. The Wings reached the second round of the playoffs before the Calgary Flames and their $36-million payroll shunted them aside in six games. When it was done, the NHL lockout came into play, wiping out 2004-05 in the process, and the league's landscape changed forever. Holland bought out Hatcher and forwards Ray Whitney and Darren McCarty to get his payroll under the new $39-million salary cap ceiling when lockout was over.

"When the CBA was announced," Holland said, "a lot of people knew they were on the bubble."

Years later, the Detroit brass looks back and recognizes that the end to those free-spending days was best for everyone.

"It's not just about Detroit – you have to think of the health of the whole league," said senior vice-president Jimmy Devellano. "The league needed to get fixed. A salary cap is better for the league and for the fans. We couldn't have unfettered salaries."

DETROIT RED WINGS

THE CONTENDERS

PAVEL BURE

2003-04 NEW YORK RANGERS: $76,488,716

The season started with right winger Pavel Bure, the team's highest-paid player at $10 million, failing his physical due to a battered knee that would end his playing days. The rest of this highly paid lot stumbled home 13th overall in the Eastern Conference, leading to a trade deadline fire sale of big-ticket players, including defenseman Brian Leetch ($6.6 million), right winger Alex Kovalev ($6.6 million) and center Petr Nedved ($4.8 million).

2002-03 NEW YORK RANGERS: $76,477,085

Bure delivered 19 goals for his $10-million salary and after the Rangers missed the playoffs for the sixth straight season, *Forbes* labelled them the most mismanaged team in hockey history.

2002-03 DALLAS STARS: $69,570,169

Dallas had been absent from the playoffs in the previous season for the first time since 1995-96, so owner Tom Hicks doled out $60 million to free agents, bringing forwards Bill Guerin and Scott Young and defenseman Philippe Boucher on board. The Stars made the playoffs, but exited via a second-round loss to the Ducks.

CHAPTER 22

BIGGEST SHOCK

2004-05 LOCKOUT

BY RORY BOYLEN

BY THE TURN OF the 21st century, work stoppages had become a semi-regular occurrence in professional sports. In football, the NFL had gone through mid-season player strikes in 1982 and 1987 that were resolved after a few weeks and didn't threaten the season. MLB had been through a number of strikes and lockouts, with its most costly stoppage coming midway through the 1994 season, when 938 games and the World Series were cancelled. And in basketball, the NBA had to shave 32 games off its regular season in 1998-99 and a 2011 lockout delayed the season opener until Christmas Day.

The NHL, of course, had its own history of a dubious relationship between players and owners. From the owners' attempts to block the formation of a players' union in the Ted Lindsay days to the shameful Alan Eagleson era, distrust had festered and led to a brief player strike in 1991-92 and a lockout in 1994-95 that lasted three-and-a-half months. The latter shaved the season down to 48 games.

Despite the history of rifts between owners and workers across professional sports, no league had allowed a dispute to erase an entire season. Even as the 2004-05 NHL lockout was cancelling games into December and January, there was still the hope that the two sides would come to some sort of agreement to save the season and have a Stanley Cup winner. After all, in '94-95 the NHL resumed games even though lawyers from both sides still wouldn't sign off on all the details until a few months later. So fans had reason to hold out hope for a solution until the bitter end, which made Gary Bettman's official cancellation of the season on Feb. 16, 2005, such a shock.

"It makes no sense to me," Tyson Nash, now retired, told THN at the time. "They aren't going to get a better deal, we aren't going to get a better deal, so why are we doing this?"

"Holy cripes! They did it," Steve Dryden, then-THN editor in chief, wrote in his notebook in the first issue after the announcement. "The doomsdayers, unlike the millennium scaremongers back in 1999, were right this time. The clock struck midnight and the world imploded. Go figure."

By the time Bettman called off the season, the lockout had been going on for nearly five months. Fans already were furious and flustered at the developments, or lack thereof, in negotiations. Because of past sports labor precedents, however, the fact that NHL

GARY BETTMAN

owners relinquished their desire for a cap a decade earlier, and the belief that reason and common sense would eventually break down propaganda and lead to business compromise, it was confounding to contemplate that a season and all its revenues had indeed been flushed away.

Even after the season was cancelled, there were still rumblings that a backdoor deal could save the season and rumors swirled that legends Wayne Gretzky and Mario Lemieux were getting involved. But nothing close to a deal-saver came to pass.

What made this dark piece of NHL history all the more shocking was how close the league and NHLPA were to an agreement on doomsday. In December, the players' union made a surprising offer to roll back salaries by 24 percent, a sum they'd refused to approach up to that point. Still, the major sticking point throughout was the league's desire for a salary cap and the union's assertion that it would go no further than offering a form of revenue sharing to aid smaller markets, a stand they would step off in mid-February, to the astonishment of some players.

Still, the union's offer was a $49-million cap that wasn't tied to league revenues. The league, meanwhile, stuck to a $42.5-million cap that would be linked to unpredictable future revenue levels. With so little between them in the dying hours, there seemed to be plenty of room for compromise and an 11th-hour signoff. To everyone's shock, however, reason was shunned and pigheaded partisanship won the day.

"A $45-million cap? Yeah, that's something I would accept if it meant we would be playing hockey and helping the game," Dwayne Roloson told THN at the time. "I know our executive committee had room to move. The league had room to move. We both had bluff hands, but nobody made the call."

The two sides finally reached a deal on a new collective bargaining agreement that July. The league got a salary cap linked to revenues, just like it wanted, and the NHLPA was left in shambles. The 2004-05 lockout left a permanent void on the Stanley Cup and remains a black mark that will never be stricken from the record books.

BIGGEST SHOCK

TESLA COIL AT THE
TAMPA BAY TIMES FORUM

THE CONTENDERS

LOCKOUT PART III

In the year leading up to the expiration of the CBA on Sept. 15, 2012, few actually believed the NHL would lock out its players again. Even after the NHLPA hired former MLBPA director Donald Fehr to lead its side, it was unbelievable to imagine a second stoppage in seven years. After all, it was thought that most of the hard work had been done in 2004-05 and only minor adjustments had to be made. Of course, it wasn't that easy and the owners shut down the league once more, though this time an agreement was reached in January 2013 in time to save the season.

RICK DIPIETRO

In 1997, the New York Islanders were slowly building an impressive young roster of prospects and players, but hasty trades and odd player personnel decisions by GM Mike Milbury stopped the team in its tracks. Take the goalie decision, for instance. In 1997, Milbury and the Islanders chose Roberto Luongo fourth overall and seemingly had an all-world starter to move forward with. Luongo played two more seasons in major junior, then split his first pro season between the Islanders and the American League. On June 24, 2000, however, Luongo was traded, along with Olli Jokinen, to the Florida Panthers for Mark Parrish and Oleg Kvasha, so that New York could select DiPietro first overall at the draft that same day. The American netminder moved straight to the NHL, but constant injuries plagued his career and resulted him being bought out of a 15-year contract after only seven seasons.

TAMPA BAY'S LIGHTNING

The Bolts' goal celebrations are shocking in the literal sense. After new owner Jeff Vinik took over the team, he invested in renovations at the Tampa Bay Times Forum. Among the upgrades were two Tesla coils in the rafters that fire forks of lightning in pre-game and goal celebrations. It's believed to be the world's largest permanent coil installation. You'll never forget whose building you're in. Just don't get too close.

CHAPTER 23

BIGGEST BANK ACCOUNT

JAROMIR JAGR

BY ROB RICHES

WHEN IT COMES TO players with the most career earnings, it shouldn't be much of a surprise to see Jaromir Jagr at the top of the list. After Jagr signed a one-year deal with the New Jersey Devils, his career contracts totalled $109,838,851 over the course of his illustrious NHL tenure. He joins MLB's Alex Rodriguez ($353,416,252), the NBA's Kevin Garnett ($340,128,663) and the NFL's Peyton Manning ($207,020,668) for the most career earnings among the Big Four professional leagues in North America.

Now, any player who has played at a consistently high level since the days before Gary Bettman became commissioner of the NHL would surely earn a big paycheque. But what makes Jagr's earnings that much more incredible is that he could have banked even more.

Jagr made a paltry $150,000 in his rookie season (1990-91), but three seasons later he'd hit seven figures. By 1999-2000, he was making more than $10 million. His pay stubs hit their zenith in 2002-03 after he signed a seven-year deal with the Washington Capitals at $11 million per season. That lasted only two seasons, however, because his league-high salary was wiped out by the 2004-05 lockout and the 24-percent rollback, as part of the collective bargaining agreement signed in the summer of 2005, brought his salary back into the seven-figure range through 2008-09. He then spent three seasons with Omsk of the Kontinental League from 2008 to 2011 where he was well compensated, but we're talking NHL totals.

Heading into 2013-14 Jagr had scored 681 goals in his NHL career, working out to $155,416.81 for each time he put the puck in the net (and each salute that would follow shortly thereafter). For each of his 1,688 points, Jagr has averaged $62,700.74, for each regular season game $76,088.32, and $523,954.71 for every playoff game. Sitting in the penalty box? He's averaged $110,363.77 per minute he's rested in the sin bin.

Jagr holds the record now, but it won't stand the test of time. Sidney Crosby ($159M), Alex Ovechkin ($135M), Shea Weber ($131M) and Zach Parise ($118M) are all set to pass Jagr in career earnings by the time their current deals expire.

JAROMIR JAGR

THE CONTENDERS

NICKLAS LIDSTROM

Second place isn't something the four-time Stanley Cup and seven-time Norris Trophy winner often experienced, but that's how it works out on this list. The Swedish blueliner earned $100,365,000 over the course of his storied career in the Motor City. He usurped Jagr when the Czech left for the KHL in 2008, but Jagr's comeback combined with Lidstrom's retirement in 2012 made that takeover brief.

CHRIS PRONGER

Another stalwart defenseman, Pronger ranks third in career earnings with $93,900,500 over stints with Hartford, St. Louis, Edmonton, Anaheim and Philadelphia. Although his career is in doubt as a result of post-concussion syndrome and a serious eye injury, Pronger will stay on the Flyers' payroll for the remaining four years of his contract, meaning he will have earned $106,050,500 by the time it expires.

JOE SAKIC

One of the pre-eminent centers of his era, Sakic earned $93,174,047 over the course of his career with the Quebec Nordiques and Colorado Avalanche. 'Burnaby Joe' truly demonstrated he was worth every cent, as he set team records for each scoring category as well as seasons and games played. Additionally, he served as captain for 16 seasons, winning two Stanley Cups along the way.

CHAPTER 24

BIGGEST CONTRACT

RICK DIPIETRO

BY AARON PORTZLINE

CHARLES WANG'S LEGACY AS owner of the New York Islanders reads like a collection of works by the spoof newspaper *The Onion:*

Islanders owner seeks sumo wrestlers to play goaltender

GM fails to turn around Islanders after 40-day tenure

Backup Islanders goaltender promoted to GM

Seriously, folks, you can't make this stuff up. But Wang's decade-long tenure as majority owner on Long Island (soon to be Brooklyn when the team moves there in 2015) has been more sad than satirical. Arguably, his most destructive act, one that reached beyond his own organization, was the signing of players to contracts that could be described as life-term, not just long-term.

Goaltender Rick DiPietro, the No. 1 overall pick by the Islanders in 2000, had played only 143 NHL games and earned 58 wins when, on Sept. 12, 2006, he signed a 15-year, $67.5-million contract. At the time, it was the longest term in NHL history. The negotiations between the Islanders and DiPietro's agent, Paul Krepelka, started months earlier with then-Islanders GM Neil Smith and culminated under Smith's replacement, Garth Snow. (Just weeks earlier, before he was promoted to GM, Snow had served as DiPietro's backup.) It was Wang, however, who pushed for the 15-year term, wanting DiPietro to be the face of the franchise until he retired.

This deal wasn't an aberration for Wang.

In the summer of 2001, shortly after center Michael Peca signed a five-year contract with the Islanders, then-GM Mike Milbury revealed he had to talk Wang out of a 10-year offer. Ultimately, Wang couldn't be stopped. Just one week after Peca's deal, the Islanders signed Alexei Yashin to a 10-year, $87.5-million contract after Milbury acquired his rights in a draft day trade with the Ottawa Senators in 2001. Five years later, Wang hadn't learned his lesson, even though the Yashin experiment bombed. It was now DiPietro's turn.

After Wang tried to sign DiPietro to a 15-year contract in 2005, the NHL strongly discouraged the deal, reportedly, so the Islanders and DiPietro settled on a one-year contract, but Wang got his wish one year later. In his defense, if DiPietro had remained healthy, maybe the contract would have made sense. He was a remarkably agile goal-

RICK DIPIETRO

tender with good puckhandling skills and a personality that sat comfortably between confident and cocky. An annual salary of $4.5 million for a goaltender with that pedigree would be a bargain.

In the first two years of the contract, DiPietro played 125 games and went 58-47-16 with eight shutouts. The Islanders were 17-21-5 when he didn't play or factor into the decision. So far, so good. But the risk of a 15-year contract reared its ugly head. Because of an unconscionable string of injuries (concussions, multiple hip and groin surgeries, torn knee ligaments and more), DiPietro played only 50 NHL games from 2008-09 through 2012-13. He'd become the face of the franchise, but not in the way Wang had intended.

On Feb. 22, 2013, the Islanders waived DiPietro and sent him to their American League affiliate, the Bridgeport Sound Tigers, where he finished the season. The Islanders bought out the remaining years of DiPietro's contract in the summer, but in the process they set another record: longest buyout in pro sports history. There were eight seasons remaining on DiPietro's contract, meaning the buyout, which lasts 16 years, will stretch until a final payment of $1.5 million is made in 2028-29. DiPietro will be 48 years old when he collects his last cheque from the Islanders.

THE CONTENDERS

ALEXEI YASHIN

Yashin was already an enigma before Wang signed him to what was at the time the richest contract in NHL history on Sept. 5, 2001. Yashin had three contract disputes in five years with Ottawa, the team that drafted him, but Wang made him an offer even he couldn't refuse: the longest term and most total money in league history at the time. Other GMs were furious.

ILYA KOVALCHUK

The New Jersey Devils' typically conservative GM, Lou Lamoriello, stepped out on July 19, 2010, with a massive contract to Kovalchuk: 17 years for $102 million. The NHL smacked Lamoriello for it, too, punishing the Devils for salary cap circumvention, because the final six seasons of the deal were all less than $1 million. The 17-year deal would have been the second-longest deal in pro sports history, behind the 25-year deal Magic Johnson signed with the NBA's Los Angeles Lakers in 1981. After the NHL killed the first contract, however, it was reconfigured into a 15-year, $100-million deal, which was set to expire in 2025 until Kovalchuk announced his retirement from the NHL in July 2013.

BOBBY HULL

Hull jumped from the NHL's Chicago Black Hawks to the Winnipeg Jets of the World Hockey Association for its inaugural season in 1972. All it took to lure 'The Golden Jet' away from the NHL was a precedent-setting contract worth $2.7 million over 10 years, including a $1-million signing bonus. It was the biggest contract ever signed in pro sports, in an era when the average NHL salary was around $20,000. Hull's deal with the Jets didn't come without grief, though. He was barred from playing for Team Canada in the Summit Series later that year and forever fractured his relationship with the Black Hawks.

CHAPTER 25

BIGGEST ENDORSEMENT EARNER

SIDNEY CROSBY

BY GEOFF KIRBYSON

EVEN IF SIDNEY CROSBY hadn't scored the gold medal-winning goal at the Vancouver Olympics in 2010, there still wouldn't have been any question about his status atop the hockey world. Not only is the Pittsburgh Penguins superstar widely regarded as the best player in the world, he's a Stanley Cup champion, a Hart Trophy winner and currently the highest-earning active NHLer from endorsements.

We've all seen him swig Gatorade, lace up his Reebok gear, reminisce about his Timbits hockey days and use a Bell Canada cellphone. He's also been spotted helping out on the sales floor at SportChek.

"Our decision to partner with Sidney was driven by the similarities between him and our brand," said Duncan Fulton, chief marketing officer of FGL Sports, which owns SportChek stores. "He knows what it takes to be the best and how much hard work is necessary to stay on top. When searching for an athlete to represent the SportChek brand, Sidney was at the top of our list."

Wayne Gretzky is far and away the all-time endorsement earner in NHL history, having accumulated almost $100 million in the 1990s alone, more than double his career NHL pay of $40,521,616. Crosby is his heir apparent, but has a long way to go to catch The Great One. His major endorsements, plus a number of others, net Crosby only about $4 million per year, according to a 2012 report by *Forbes*, which is less than half of his $8.7-million annual NHL salary.

While NHLers' salaries are made public, neither players nor the companies that sponsor them are under any obligation to reveal what any endorsement deal is worth. Sources told The Hockey News in 2010 that Crosby's contract with Reebok was worth nearly $10 million over the next seven years, or roughly $1.4 million annually.

No figures were available for the deals Crosby has with other brands, but you can bet Tim Hortons was eager to hook up with 'Sid the Kid.' The coffee chain has long positioned itself as the place where hockey moms and dads get their coffee before early morning practices. Adding Crosby to the mix has only reinforced that relationship.

"Our customers feel that Sidney is this generation's iconic representation of the game," said Rob Forbes, senior director of marketing and national programs at Tim Hortons. "When you add to that the fact that Sidney got his start as a Timbits hockey player, there is a very natural and genuine link between him and our brand."

THE CONTENDERS

ALEX OVECHKIN

The Washington Capitals right winger is No. 2 on the off-ice earnings list with $2.5 million thanks to deals with Nike, Bauer and Gatorade. The three-time Hart Trophy winner is also the face of Gillette. One of the stipulations of his contract is that he be clean-shaven during the season, except during Movember, when he can grow a moustache, and the playoffs, when most players grow beards.

JONATHAN TOEWS

The Chicago Blackhawks captain comes in at No. 3 with the $1.2 million he earned last year as a spokesman for brands such as Canadian Tire, Bauer, Chevrolet and Lemonhead. These companies have hitched their wagon to a player with an unparalleled resume for someone just 25 years old: two Stanley Cups, one Olympic gold, one World Championship gold and two world juniors gold medals.

STEVEN STAMKOS

If Stamkos ever brought the game's best hair to a hockey market, he'd be a cinch to crack the seven-figure club. The Tampa Bay Lightning center sits No. 4 with $800,000 annually thanks to deals with Nike, Bauer and Tissot.

CHAPTER 26

BIGGEST SHOWMAN

ALEX OVECHKIN

BY MICHAEL TRAIKOS

THERE WAS THE TIME he scored his 50th goal and celebrated by dropping his stick and pretending it was on fire. There was the time he showed up at the 2010 Olympics wearing skates adorned with his signature yellow laces and what looked like a red-eyed sheep with his No. 8 painted over a backdrop of flames just above the blades. And there was the time at the 2009 All-Star Game skills competition when he donned oversized sunglasses and a fishing hat and, after taking a squirt of Gatorade, used two sticks for a shootout attempt.

But the thing that makes Alex Ovechkin a hot dog – the kind you smother with mustard, sauerkraut and all the fixings – is his jumping. The Washington Capitals sniper isn't the first to finish a goal by skating hard toward the nearest boards and bodychecking the glass. What has become hockey's version of the Lambeau Leap, however, he's made his own.

"It's like a playoff goal," said teammate Karl Alzner. "Guys jump off the glass after scoring a goal in the playoffs, because there's so much pressure and they're so happy. Well, Alex seems to do that all the time, not just the playoffs. It gets us fired up."

Since Ovechkin arrived in the NHL in 2005-06, with a tinted visor and a cartoon-like personality, he's scored more than any other player from that season on. As a 20-year-old, he won the Calder Trophy with a 52-goal, 106-point season. Two years later, he scored 65 goals, the most since Mario Lemieux scored 69 in 1995-96, and won his first of three Hart Trophies. In 601 games through his first eight seasons, he had 371 goals.

And yet, when Ovechkin scores, it's like he's scoring for the first time. It's pure joy. Like he's back playing bantam in Russia in a small arena with only family members in the stands. To some, it might seem like he's showboating or thinking only of himself and his stats. But if he could, Ovechkin would gladly jump through that glass and celebrate with every fan in the building.

That smile, gap-toothed and stretching across his face like some Jim Carrey character, is infectious. When he smiles, you can't help but smile yourself. And that's what he wants. He wants you to have as much fun watching as he is having playing. To watch Ovechkin is to watch a video game. He does things that defy logic and physics. And he makes it look easy.

"In games he likes to do things and try things that you would only ever try in practice or I would only ever try in summer hockey practice," Alzner said. "He's got the confidence to go out there and do the things that you wouldn't expect. That's why a lot of times it works, because players on other teams don't expect him to try it."

In a 2009 game against the Montreal Canadiens, Ovechkin intercepted a pass and, with Roman Hamrlik skating toward him, banked the puck off the boards, spun around the Habs defenseman to avoid the check and sprung toward the goal. As if that weren't enough, Ovechkin completed the play by getting dragged to the ice and scoring from the seat of his pants.

"I knew he was going to do something," Hamrlik said. "But I didn't know he was going to do a 360 and bounce over the boards and beat me. Unfortunately for me, he ended up scoring the goal."

"HE'S GOT THE CONFIDENCE TO GO OUT THERE AND DO THE THINGS THAT YOU WOULDN'T EXPECT. THAT'S WHY A LOT OF TIMES IT WORKS, BECAUSE PLAYERS ON OTHER TEAMS DON'T EXPECT HIM TO TRY IT"

For most players, that goal would have defined their career. But Ovechkin, whose highlights could be a paid exhibit, scored his Mona Lisa as a rookie against the Phoenix Coyotes in 2006. Stealing the puck at center ice, he skated toward Paul Mara and dragged the puck through the Coyotes defenseman's skates. Mara stuck with Ovechkin, put him on his back and assumed that was the end of it. Ovechkin, however, never gave up. Sliding on his back, he somehow slid the puck past goaltender Brian Boucher.

"My first reaction when I see it on the replay is 'Wow! What I do? How I did it?' " Ovechkin said at the time. "The goal is a kind of lucky goal, but it was beautiful."

"Beautiful" is a nice way of describing Ovechkin's personality. In a league where players are hidden behind helmets and visors and layers upon layers of protective equipment, and the one thing that separates Sidney Crosby from the rest of the pack is work ethic, Ovechkin stands out. Even without the oversized sunglasses, he's larger than life. You can

BIGGEST SHOWMAN

ALEX OVECHKIN

see it on the ice with his willingness to try the unimaginable. And you can definitely see it off the ice with his ventures into hip-hop, surreal Mr. Big chocolate bar commercials and an even bigger lifestyle.

"He's got a loud personality," Alzner said. "He talks loud and he likes to make noise. He's got a bit of an aura around him. When he walks into the room everyone takes notice of him and watches what he's up to. Even when he's got his headphones on, he's singing loud so that we can hear him. He drives fancy cars, has nice watches. He's just one of those guys that when you see him, you're like, 'Holy smokes, this guy's at the top.' "

THE CONTENDERS

TEEMU SELANNE

'The Finnish Flash' has toned down his act as he's gotten older, but when he stepped into the league with the Winnipeg Jets as a fresh-faced rookie in 1992-93 he was an instant showman. After breaking Mike Bossy's single-season record for goals by a rookie with his 54th (Selanne finished the season with 76), the Jets' right winger tossed his glove in the air and proceeded to use his stick as a gun to shoot it down. It's easily the best goal celebration of all-time.

PATRICK KANE

When you talk about Kane, you have to start with the mullet. To have one in the 1980s was normal. Today it's a joke. But for someone who once donned a Superman cape and black-rimmed glasses for the shootout competition at an All-Star Game, it's also a hint that he wants to be noticed. And with an arsenal that includes spin-o-ramas, Datsyukian dekes and ankle-breaking toe drags, Kane delivers.

PAVEL BURE

It's difficult to say whether Bure was a hot dog or just so skilled that his speed and jaw-dropping skill made it look like he was trying to put on a show. Either way, 'The Russian Rocket' was something special. Going top speed on a breakaway, he didn't just beat a goalie with a shot or a simple deke. No, he would self-pass the puck off the inside of his skate and then go upstairs just for the heck of it.

BIGGEST SHOWMAN

PATRICK KANE

CHAPTER 27

BIGGEST FLASH IN THE PAN

JACQUES RICHARD

BY RORY BOYLEN

CONVENTIONAL WISDOM IN HOCKEY dictates it's always safer to move a player's development along slowly, rather than rush him into the NHL spotlight before he's ready. Yet these mistakes have been made throughout history and likely always will be.

For instance, when the expansion Atlanta Thrashers chose Patrik Stefan with their first-ever draft pick, No. 1 overall in 1999, they put him immediately in the NHL and helplessly watched him fail to live up to his potential as a professional. But despite being a first-year franchise, the team was repeating history and making the same mistake a deposed Atlanta franchise had made 27 years prior.

When Jacques Richard was starring alongside Guy Lafleur for the Quebec Remparts in the Quebec League in the early 1970s, NHL teams salivated at his potential. He'd put up 239 points over two years with Lafleur and had set a career high with 71 goals and 160 points in his last junior year after the future Hall of Famer had moved on to the NHL. Richard's offense and speed were at an elite level and his last name added to the promise and mystique around his future. But that's about all Richard had in common with 'The Rocket' or 'The Pocket Rocket.'

Richard was a stud prospect who some believed would be as good or possibly even better than Lafleur. Two expansion teams were entering the NHL in 1972-73 and, after the New York Islanders scooped Billy Harris with the first-overall pick, the Atlanta Flames went with Richard.

Confidence immediately became an issue for the young francophone, who needed a translator to do interviews. He was shy, which, according to teammate Phil Myre, stalled his desire to learn the language.

"He's afraid somebody will make fun of him," Myre told The Hockey News in 1972. "He knows a little English, but he's too bashful to speak it."

In training camp that year, Richard had trouble keeping his head up playing in a much faster style of game. Time and again his coaches had to drill him to look ahead and instruct the rest of the Flames to tone it down and not catch him in the middle of the ice. That didn't stop sturdy blueliner and teammate Bob Paradise from clobbering Richard in

BIGGEST FLASH IN THE PAN

JACQUES RICHARD

one scrimmage, though, leaving the rookie writhing in pain on the ice.

"I've just been disappointed in myself because I know I can do better than what I've done," Richard told THN that fall. "I just need to get confidence in myself."

Even after Harris outscored Richard in points 50 to 31 that season, there was little doubt Richard was destined to be a superstar one day. He only eclipsed 50 points once, however, and that didn't come until the tail end of a short, disappointing career.

Richard lasted three years in Atlanta, topping out at 27 goals and 43 points, before he was shipped to the Buffalo Sabres. He spent parts of four seasons in that organization, in the American League nearly half the time, and after failing to improve his defensive game or establish himself as an NHL scorer he was released by the Sabres and signed with the Quebec Nordiques.

At this point in Richard's career, not much was expected of him. While his on-ice struggles were well documented and easy to see, behind-the-scenes factors were also conspiring against him. Alcohol, drug and gambling issues eroded his focus and skill set, and were problems that followed him into retirement. But in 1980-81, Richard's first full season with his hometown Nordiques, he finally showed a flash of the player he was supposed to be with the Flames. Coach Michel Bergeron put him on a line with brothers Peter and Anton Stastny and watched him become perhaps the most unlikely 50-goal scorer in NHL history. With 52 goals and 103 points, Richard was suddenly a top-10 scorer on one of the most dynamic lines in the league and at 28 he still had plenty of time to realize at least some of his vast potential.

As quickly as he captured that lightning, though, it was gone in a flash. Richard slumped to 15 goals and 41 points in 1981-82 and slowed even more the following season, which resulted in his demotion to the Fredericton Express of the AHL. After that, the former phenom disappeared from the professional hockey scene altogether. He was just 31 years old.

A troubled lifestyle followed Richard. In 1989, he was caught smuggling approximately five pounds of cocaine in his golf bag when he returned from a trip to Columbia, for which he was imprisoned seven years.

Richard died in the late hours of Oct. 8, 2002, when his car struck a culvert, killing him instantly. He was one day removed from his 50th birthday.

THE CONTENDERS

KEN HODGE JR.

A second generation NHLer, Hodge Jr. didn't come close to having the same staying power as his father. He only scored 87 points in his career, 42 percent of which came in one season. A third-round pick of the Minnesota North Stars in 1984, Hodge Jr. had his only full NHL season in 1990-91 with the Boston Bruins, when he notched 30 goals and 59 points. The following year he struggled, with six goals and 17 points in 42 games. After a brief 25-game stint with the expansion Tampa Bay Lightning in 1992-93, he never saw NHL action again.

SCOTT BJUGSTAD

Bjugstad was a standout at the Minnesota high school level and with the University of Minnesota before being drafted in the ninth round by the North Stars in 1981. He scored 11 goals in his rookie season and was never projected to be an offensive star, which made his sophomore performance all the more surprising. That year, Bjugstad was put on the team's top line with Neal Broten and Dino Ciccarelli and exploded with 43 goals and 76 points. But Bjugstad scored only 14 goals total over the next two seasons combined and accumulated only 53 more points the rest of his NHL career.

JIM CAREY

Perhaps the most famous one-and-done, Carey actually had two impressive seasons in professional hockey. The first came in 1994-95, when he posted a 2.76 goals-against average and .909 save percentage with the Portland Pirates of the AHL and won the Baz Bastien Award for best goalie in the league. He also shone in 28 games with the Washington Capitals after the lockout, with a 2.13 goals-against average and .913 save percentage. In 1995-96, however, Carey took the NHL by storm, winning 35 games with a 2.26 GAA and .906 SP, earning the Vezina Trophy as a 22-year-old. His stats declined the following season, though, and he was traded to the Boston Bruins. Carey was out of hockey before the turn of the millennium.

CHAPTER 28

BIGGEST BRAIN

SCOTTY BOWMAN

BY WAYNE FISH

NOTHING EVER GOT PAST Scotty Bowman. Not other coaches' attempts at line-matchup deception, not the latest news on some hotshot junior player, not the newest trends in offense or defense. And definitely not some semi-devious players' attempts to circumvent curfew on the road.

Case in point: Bowman was coaching the Montreal Canadiens in the 1970s and the team was on a road trip that made a stop in Los Angeles. Bowman suspected some players were taking advantage of the nightlife in the City of Angels. But rather than hide behind a potted plant in the hotel lobby to check on his charges, Bowman enlisted the help of the doorman. He handed the guy a hockey stick, along with $10, and told him to ask each player who showed up after 11 p.m. to sign it.

Pierre McGuire, an assistant under Bowman with the Stanley Cup-champion Pittsburgh Penguins in 1992, can take it from there:

"So four or five big-name players signed the stick. Bowman has the stick when they get on the bus the next morning and he says, 'OK, any of you break curfew?' And they were all like, 'Oh, no, no, no.' And Bowman goes, 'Well, everyone who signed this stick…' and he starts reading off the names… 'just broke curfew, so you owe me.' He said the team went up to Oakland that day and they played an unbelievable game, because all the guys knew they were in deep trouble."

That story is typical of the imaginative thinking that made Bowman the best there's ever been when it comes to translating strategy into success. He not only won nine Stanley Cups with three different teams (no other coach has won with more than two), he changed the game with his attention to detail and constant emphasis on preparation. Disciples such as Mike Keenan, a Stanley Cup champion with one team (1994 Rangers) and finalist with two others, have made no secret of the fact that they employed aspects of Bowman's coaching style.

When asked if a few of those Bowman principles rubbed off on McGuire, the former Hartford Whalers coach and current NBC hockey analyst didn't hesitate to reply.

"Always be prepared," McGuire said. "Watch as much as you can, learn as much as you can. Don't be afraid to ask probing questions. Don't think you know everything. Keep

BIGGEST BRAIN

SCOTTY BOWMAN

your ears open, learn something new every day."

Bowman learned and then put theory into practice. He was an innovator, thinking outside the box. He tried new stuff, like putting out four defensemen on the penalty kill. Whereas other coaches instructed their players to shoot low in practice to protect the goalie, Bowman offered no such favor to his netminders, because he wanted his drills to simulate game conditions.

Bowman was no softer on rookies. Mike Knuble showed up on the Detroit Red Wings roster as a freshman in 1996-97 and won his only Stanley Cup ring the following season under Bowman. It was an intimidating time for Knuble, but a valuable learning period.

"IF HE WANTED TO MAKE AN ADJUSTMENT, HE DIDN'T HAVE TO SAY ANYTHING. HE WOULD JUST CHANGE HIS ICE TIME OR A LINEMATE TO GET A PLAYER MOTIVATED"

"I was one of the 'Black Aces' during the '97 playoffs and in practice we were working on some kind of play," Knuble said. "If I remember right, it was a drill where we were trying to knock a pass out of the air. Bowman stops the play and after (a miss by another player), he said, 'Even Mike Knuble can knock that one down.' And I was like, 'Oh-h-h-h.' You just put your head down and line up again. That was a little bit of a stinger."

But in the end, the good far outweighed the bad. Knuble, a University of Michigan graduate, is a student of the game and the lessons learned from Bowman helped keep his career going past his 40th birthday. Learning discipline at an early age has proven invaluable.

"If he wanted to make an adjustment, he didn't have to say anything," Knuble said. "He would just change his ice time or a linemate to get a player motivated."

Or get a hockey stick signed in the middle of the night.

BILL TORREY

THE CONTENDERS

SAM POLLOCK

Pollock, architect of the '60s and '70s Canadiens dynasties, is acknowledged as one of the greatest talent evaluators ever to grace the game. Pollock won 12 Stanley Cups (nine as GM) and was a shrewd trader. His finest hour came when he held the inept California Golden Seals' No. 1 pick in 1971. Pollock traded the valuable Ralph Backstrom to the equally bad Los Angeles Kings late in the regular season to make sure the Seals finished last. The player Pollock took in the draft: Guy Lafleur.

BILL TORREY

Torrey was the mastermind of the 1980s Islanders dynasty that won four straight Cups, the most consecutive by any U.S.-based team. And he was equal to the wiles of other brilliant brains in the game. When Torrey selected Denis Potvin with the No. 1 pick in 1973, Pollock came calling with a tempting package of valuable veteran players for the dynamic defenseman. But Torrey would have none of it. He went on to draft future Hall of Famers Bryan Trottier and Mike Bossy, key cogs in the Islanders' run in the early '80s.

TOE BLAKE

His five Cups in a row with Montreal in the 1950s set a record that will probably never be broken. Teams like the '70s Canadiens and '80s Islanders and Oilers tried, but all fell short. Many believe the decision to hire Blake in 1955 to keep Maurice Richard under control after the 1955 riots played a big part in launching Montreal's late '50s run of dominance. Blake won a total of eight Cups as a coach and three as a player, captaining the '44 and '46 Canadiens to championships and winning the Hart Trophy in 1938-39.

CHAPTER 29

BIGGEST TASKMASTER

EDDIE SHORE

BY STAN FISCHLER

THERE WAS NO TOUGHER defenseman in NHL history than famed hitter Eddie Shore, who starred for the Boston Bruins. When he bought the American League's Springfield Indians for $42,000, however, he soon proved a tougher taskmaster as an owner than as a walloper of opposing players.

Shore's reputation as a martinet owner in the '50s and '60s was so scary that players would insist on a contract clause that under no circumstances could they be traded to Springfield. Larry Hillman, who played for Shore in 1962-63, could vouch for that.

"It was like being sentenced to a year in Siberia," he said.

How bad? For one thing, players had to ask Shore's permission to butter their toast and he had them drinking water with a lot of iodine in it to kill germs. He often fined players for being 10 minutes late when their watches accurately reported they were 10 minutes early.

"My time is the *only* time," 'The Boss' barked. Adjusting therefore to 'Shore Time,' the players had to keep their watches a half-hour ahead.

Shore levied a $200 fine against any player who slept on the team bus. He opened training camp by having players execute delicate ballet steps followed by tap dancing. He once locked a referee in the dressing room as punishment for what he considered poor officiating. Players who were scratched from the lineup had to make popcorn, blow up balloons and sell programs at Eastern States Coliseum until they were back on the varsity. Defenseman Don Johns was even advised by Shore that he wasn't combing his hair correctly.

"Eddie told me to part it on the other side," Johns said. "That way it would help because I'd have something to think about."

Shore was equally tough on goaltenders who were ordered not to fall to the ice.

"If a goalie went down to block a shot during practice," said ex-Springfield goalie Don Simmons, "Shore would get a piece of twine and tie the goalie's arm to the crossbar of the net. Then he'd dare him to fall."

Shore's machinations eventually became so severe that in 1967-68 his Indians revolted and hired Toronto attorney Alan Eagleson to represent them. Shore eventually yielded to the pressure and delivered control of his team to the Los Angeles Kings. That decision inspired NHL players to contact Eagleson, which led to the formation of the NHL Players' Association.

BIGGEST TASKMASTER

EDDIE SHORE

THE CONTENDERS

CONN SMYTHE

The Toronto Maple Leafs boss served as an officer in the First and Second World Wars. Not surprisingly, Smythe ruled his hockey team with militaristic discipline. Break a Smythe rule and beware the brig, Maple Leaf Gardens variety. When 'The Little Major' thought three-time Cup-winning right winger Bill Ezinicki was too interested in golf, he dealt 'Wild Bill' to Boston. When his premier penalty killer, Johnny McCormack, got married mid-season, 'Goose' was eventually sold to the Montreal Canadiens. Referees got grief from Smythe as well. Disturbed by Clarence Campbell's officiating prior to the Second World War, Smythe had him permanently removed from the ice.

JOHN TORTORELLA

There's never a question of the pecking order when Tortorella coaches. Even stars aren't free from his infamous fury, as Brad Richards found out when he was benched by Tortorella during the 2013 playoffs. The two had even won a Stanley Cup together in 2004, with Richards taking Conn Smythe honors.

Tortorella's memory is as short as his fuse. His struggles with superstars date back to his first head coaching job in the NHL. At the time Tortorella took over as coach of the Tampa Bay Lightning, young Vincent Lecavalier was the club's marquee player and first in just about everything, even when it came to preferred parking outside the arena. When Tortorella moved into his new digs, he immediately annexed Lecavalier's lane and there was no veto allowed for the star. 'Torts' was the boss and therefore got the space.

PUNCH IMLACH

Legend has it the only reason Imlach's Maple Leafs won four Stanley Cups in six years (1962 to 1967) was that his players hated him so much they won titles just to show up their coach-GM. One by one, Imlach's biggest stars were turned off by his unpleasantness, even in happy times. When Toronto beat the Chicago Black Hawks in 1962 to win its first of three straight Cups, Imlach angrily ordered his troops to stop taking celebratory photos and get right out of the dressing room. Imlach's irritable behavior gave Frank Mahovlich a nervous breakdown and inspired Carl Brewer to walk out on the team, among many other negative reactions to Imlach.

CHAPTER 30

BIGGEST MOMENT

1967 EXPANSION

BY JAY GREENBERG

NOTHING EVER HAS CHANGED hockey to the degree the great expansion of 1967 did. And having anticipated that effect, NHL owners jumped into the project more reluctantly than the bold increase suggested.

While other sports were spending the 1960s growing franchises in the Pacific time zone, Chicago Black Hawks owner James Norris was downing suggestions that NHL teams in Los Angeles and the Bay Area would make a league already playing to over 95-percent capacity any more popular.

"This would mean we'd lose four games with the Maple Leafs and Canadiens," Norris said.

He and his brother Bruce, owner of the Detroit Red Wings, weren't the only anti-expansionists.

"New York and Boston (then perennial doormats) keep drawing because there are only six teams in the league," said Toronto owner Conn Smythe. "Two more teams would make 10 more bad games."

But Smythe's son, Stafford, elevated to the Maple Leafs' presidency in 1961, felt differently from his father, joining Montreal owner David Molson and New York Rangers president Bill Jennings, who would chair the expansion committee, in a desire to add teams. With Western League owners talking about declaring themselves a major league and starting a bidding war on players, the NHL's choice – begin paying dramatically more for talent or make money in television and expansion fees – became a no-brainer arguing for the addition of more than just two teams on the West Coast.

The plan was borrowed from Branch Rickey, the legendary baseball executive. Rickey had teamed with William Shea, jilted Brooklyn Dodgers fan and politically influential New York lawyer, in efforts to bring a second baseball team back to New York to replace the Dodgers and Giants. Investors of the Continental League, using an implied threat to form their own competing venture, were working to become a third major league. The American and National Leagues ended that threat by adding four teams, including ones in Los Angeles and New York in the early '60s.

But the concept of an entirely new division, competitive within itself, was attractive to old-guard NHL owners like the Norrises, who had no interest in diminishing their existing rivalries with too many games against new teams. Norris had another selfish incentive: dumping the decrepit St. Louis Arena, which the Black Hawks had bought to house a Central League team, to a new NHL tenant. Thus by 1965, NHL president Clarence Campbell had stopped dismissing expansion as "columnist talk" and growth had become inevitable.

In February 1966, applicants from Baltimore, Philadelphia, Buffalo, Vancouver, Louisville, Minneapolis-St. Paul, Cleveland, two from Pittsburgh, two from the Bay Area and four from Los Angeles arrived at the Plaza Hotel in New York for two days of interviews. At those meetings, franchises were granted to groups that had new arenas or at least blueprints for them.

Jack Kent Cooke, building the palatial Forum in suburban Inglewood, Calif., beat out Los Angeles Rams owner Dan Reeves along with Reeves' co-owner of the Western League's Los Angeles Blades, Jim Piggott, who proposed to play in the seven-year-old Los Angeles Memorial Sports Arena.

Barend van Gerbig's group had purchased the San Francisco Seals prior to their final WHL season of 1966-67 and before they'd moved to Oakland, with the intention of getting on board with the NHL a season later. Van Gerbig, a New York Wall Street tycoon with ownership stakes in Union Carbide and Standard Oil, led a group of more than 50 partners and got his wish when he was awarded an NHL franchise.

Pittsburgh, with a six-year-old Civic Arena and a short history of sound support for its American League Hornets, had been a virtual lock and that franchise went to a local group headed by Pennsylvania state senator Jack McGregor.

Walter Bush, a lawyer prominent in Twin Cities amateur hockey circles and part owner of the Central League's Minneapolis Bruins, teamed with Gordon Ritz, a construction company owner and former player at Yale, to win a Minnesota franchise with its facility to be built across the parking lot from the stadium of the well-supported baseball Twins in Bloomington.

Eagles owner Jerry Wolman's plan to build a new 15,000-plus-seat arena in South Philadelphia was kept secret until the night before the franchises were awarded. Even without a minor league team, Philadelphia surprisingly beat out Baltimore, which had a thriving AHL franchise, but a Civic Center that seated only 11,000.

Norris' determination to rid himself of the St. Louis Arena wasn't deterred. Despite no bids from that city for a franchise, one was granted conditionally regardless and eventually purchased by Sidney Saloman III.

Because Smythe didn't want a team within a two-hour drive, Buffalo never had a chance. Neither did Vancouver, despite its new Pacific Coliseum, because another Canadian franchise wouldn't advance the league's U.S. television objectives. But in prioritizing markets and arenas, the league paid the first of many heavy prices in poor ownerships.

Wolman proved to be overextended and partners Ed Snider and Bill Putnam didn't secure the $2 million to pay the Flyers' franchise fee until the day of the expansion draft. The Pittsburgh Penguins, whose multiple owners were drained by another startup venture in soccer, had to be sold by the end of the first season to Detroit businessman

Donald Parsons. A gleaming arena just outside blue-collar Oakland quickly proved unable to attract fans from San Francisco and subsequent ownership was in receivership by the end of Year 3.

The league, true to its objective, had its coveted national game of the week on CBS. Players buried in the minor leagues, many of them overdue for an opportunity, were suddenly major-leaguers and salaries were about to begin an unalterable climb. But the NHL brand wasn't instantly creating many more fans than had been supporting the minor league teams in the added cities. So with the new franchises in need of cash, another expansion came in 1970.

By that time, threats for more Canadian content in the league by parliament and Vancouver's failed efforts to get the Seals had made that city the next obvious choice. And with terrible attendance in Oakland, Pittsburgh and Los Angeles, the promise of a sold-out, refurbished Auditorium in near-to-Canada Buffalo also became attractive.

The new teams' ability to win 33 percent of the points in their four games, each against established teams, made Campbell's prediction of parity within five years seem prescient at first. But the West's success against the East declined in Year 2, then again in Year 3. Under the direction of their dynamic young coach Scott Bowman, the St. Louis Blues had quickly dwarfed their expansion brethren, but nevertheless failed to win a game against Montreal twice and then Boston in the first three Stanley Cup finals of the expansion era. But those bad finals, which ended when Chicago transferred to the West as Vancouver and Buffalo came in, were only the surface wounds of worsening competitive problems.

The star players were all in the east, including Boston's Bobby Orr, the revolutionary rushing defenseman who, along with groundbreaking center Phil Esposito, feasted on the declining level of competition. In the second year of expansion, Esposito wasn't only the first NHL scorer to break 100 points (he finished with 126, a whopping 39 more than league leader Stan Mikita had the year before), but also one of three who broke the barrier.

The universal amateur draft, which began in 1969 as NHL team sponsorship of junior clubs ended, gave the weakest clubs the first picks and opportunities to gain parity. But most of the new teams squandered their ability to catch up by their willingness to trade high picks, principally to Montreal GM Sam Pollock, who was building a late 1970s dynasty off the backs of the struggling expansion teams. Only Philadelphia refused to sell off its future and became the building model. When in Year 7 Ed Snider's Flyers became the first expansion team to win the Stanley Cup, not one of the other 1967-born teams had a winning record. The Sabres, who the Flyers beat for their second consecutive title in 1975, and the Islanders, who had a winning record by Year 3 on the way to four consecutive Cups, joined Philadelphia as the only expansion teams justifying the league's growth.

Nevertheless, the problems of the 1967 cities failed to deter the creation of the new World Hockey Association, which in turn motivated the NHL to beat the new league into new buildings in Atlanta and on Long Island in 1972. For the same reason, Kansas City and Washington were added in 1974 to bring the NHL to 18 teams.

By then, Pittsburgh was a year away from bankruptcy, the Seals were being operated by the

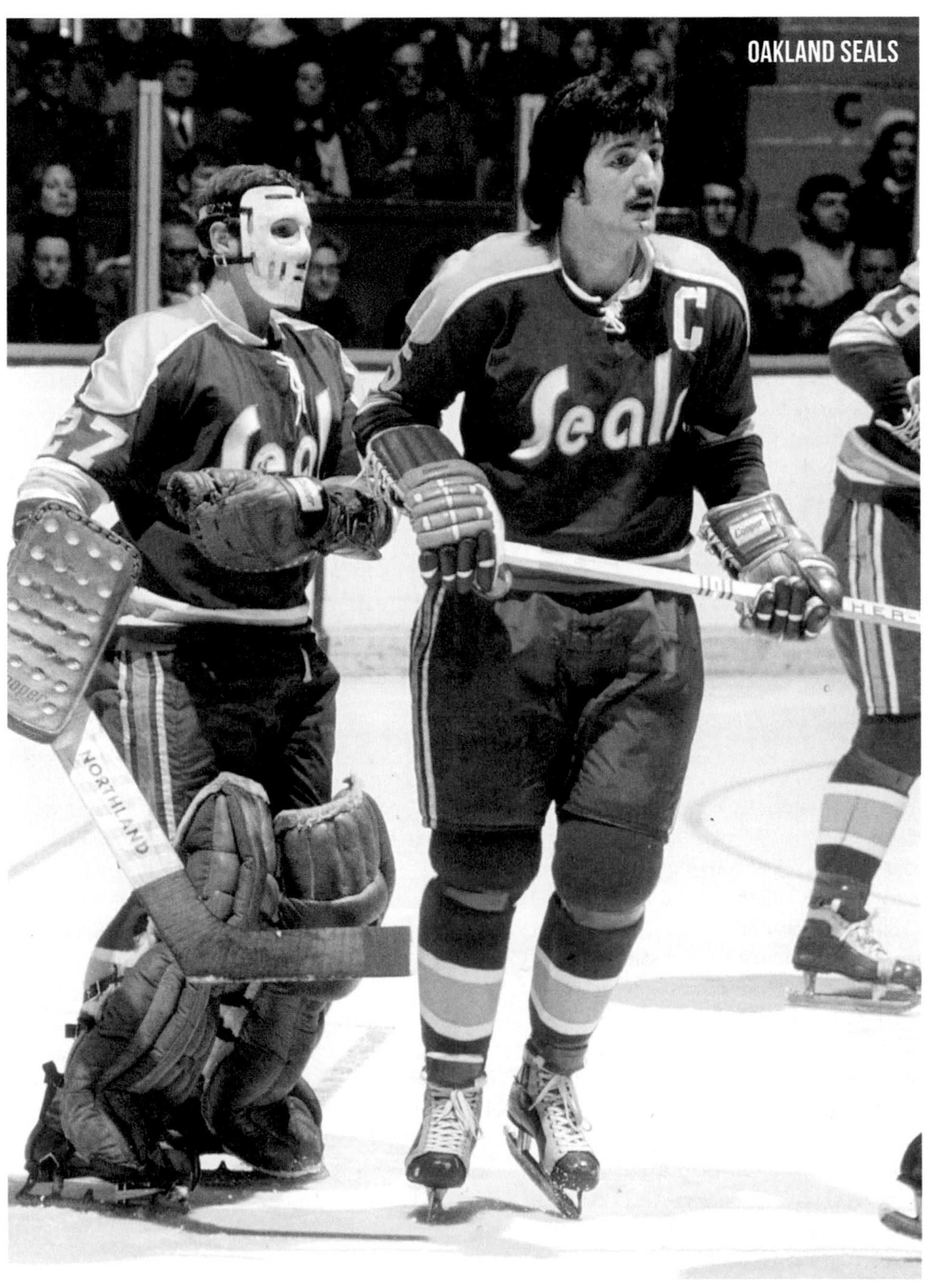
OAKLAND SEALS
Seals
Seals
27
NORTHLAND

league and the WHA's own struggles cancelled the urgency for another expansion to Denver and Seattle in 1976, though Denver would get the failed Kansas City team a year later.

By 1975, NBC, which had replaced CBS as the national carrier, dropped the NHL, which would wait until the 1980s for programming-hungry, fledgling local cable operations to save the sport on television. That was too late to keep the Flames from leaving Atlanta for Calgary, the Colorado Rockies from dumping Denver for the New Jersey Meadowlands and the Seals from abandoning Oakland for Cleveland, where after two seasons they became the only franchise of the four major sports during the 20th century to actually fold. Their roster then merged with the struggling Minnesota North Stars.

It was a rough go through the 1970s for a league too needy of expansion cash that had put too many franchises in the hands of too many wrong people. Even as the Islanders were putting together a dynasty, owner Roy Boe was defaulting on obligations, forcing a sale to a group led by John Pickett.

The next expansion, in 1979, was one of financial sense, eliminating the competition by

“NEW YORK AND BOSTON (THEN PERENNIAL DOORMATS) KEEP DRAWING BECAUSE THERE ARE ONLY SIX TEAMS IN THE LEAGUE. TWO MORE TEAMS WOULD MAKE 10 MORE BAD GAMES”

bringing in four WHA teams from smaller, hockey-happy markets. But 18 years later, all those franchises except Edmonton had moved into larger markets that were the original inspiration for expansion. Never mind that 46 years and seven teams in the Sunbelt later, national television has yet to justify the expansion effort and probably never will.

The league, still chasing immediate expansion cash under the guise of adding television markets, brought in teams 27-30 from 1998 to 2000 by promising the new owners labor 'cost certainty.'

By 2004-05, rather than allowing market forces to doom teams that couldn't afford $50 to $60-million payrolls, a salary cap became the mandate for a lockout that had nothing to do with competitive balance, since there wasn't one repeat semifinalist in the three years prior to the work stoppage. There were more good players than ever before and still not enough to go around, so coaches spread what they had over four lines and played not to lose, draining excitement from the game even as failed markets like the Bay Area, Minnesota, Denver and Atlanta were brought back into the league under more stable ownerships and before bigger crowds.

Through trial and error of eight franchise relocations, a 1994 lockout that took away half a season and a 2004-05 lockout that wiped out an entire one, the sport has relatively thrived, playing to 91-percent capacity in 2006-07, close to what it achieved in 1966-67. The game is faster, but scoring is closer to what it was in 1967 than in the 21-team '80s when the level of play was the best ever.

The San Jose Sharks, Tampa Bay Lightning, Ottawa Senators and Florida Panthers learned from the hard lessons of earlier expansion teams. Draft hauls had become thinner and, unfortunately, the spectacular accident of a number of great players landing on one of them and creating a memorable dynasty has become less likely.

Of course, Wayne Gretzky, Mario Lemieux and Sidney Crosby would have found jobs even in a six-team league and the sport would not have been denied their brilliance. But if hockey's version of George Bailey, in a fit of Christmas Eve depression, was shown by an angel what the NHL would be like if it had failed to expand, legendary teams like the Philadelphia's Broad Street Bullies and the Islanders and Oilers of the '80s would never have existed.

In 1967, Tommy Williams was the only American-born player in the NHL. In 1996, a team of American NHLers beat Canada's best in the World Cup. New professional role models had inspired more future pros on the grassroots level from Minnesota down through even Sunbelt cities and the demand for talent and wins pushed NHL teams to look to Europe for what became some of its greatest stars.

Canada, stilt caretakers of the soul of the game, has franchises in Edmonton, Calgary and Ottawa that would never have existed without the forces that brought about expansion. But Winnipeg and Quebec City, just as rabid, subsequently lost teams for the same rcasons, though Winnipeg eventually returned.

Millions of fans have been created and, most important, so have countless thrills. From 1967, every decision of the league to add teams was a financial one. But the true bottom line in sports has always been moments and memories, ultimately justifying every expansion decision, both good and bad, the NHL has ever made.

THE CONTENDERS

50 IN 50

Every year, the NHL's top goal scorer is awarded a trophy named in honor of this Hall of Famer and for good reason. Maurice Richard was the first NHLer to reach the 50-goal plateau, attaining it in 50 games in 1944-45. In reaching the mark, Richard ushered in the milestone era in which players set their sights on season and career targets. Only four others have officially reached 50 in 50: Mike Bossy, Wayne Gretzky, Mario Lemieux and Brett Hull. It stands as the ultimate benchmark for goal-scoring supremacy.

GORDIE HOWE UNRETIRES

He was 45, a year removed from induction into the Hall of Fame and had begun his second career working in the Red Wings front office. But when the WHA's Houston Aeros offered Howe a contract to join his sons Mark and Marty on the ice, the 25-year NHL veteran chose to return. Howe underwent surgery to repair the wrist that forced his initial retirement and went on to finish third in league scoring with 100 points. He led the Aeros to the Avco Cup in his first two seasons, playing six total in the WHA before a final stop in the NHL and retiring for good at 52.

SIDNEY CROSBY'S CONCUSSION

It was the hit heard around the hockey world, though the fallout was at first minimal. After David Steckel clipped Crosby at the 2011 Winter Classic, Crosby got up slowly and looked groggy, but briefly returned to the game and was even cleared to play in the next against the Tampa Bay Lightning. A follow-up hit from the Bolts' Victor Hedman, however, knocked him out for the season, the playoffs and the start of 2011-12. It was later revealed that Crosby had sustained a concussion in the Steckel collision. As whispers of retirement dogged him throughout his recovery, Crosby became an outspoken critic of the NHL's lack of protection for players, which began the league's trend toward banning headshots.

CHAPTER 31

BIGGEST SAVE

JACQUES PLANTE

BY SARAH McLELLAN

THE SAVE WAS IMPORTANT. And iconic. And innovative. It was also, arguably, accidental.

If he could have wielded his blocker or kicked up his pads or positioned his Montreal Canadiens logo to absorb the puck, goaltender Jacques Plante likely would have. Instead, a rising backhand from New York Rangers star Andy Bathgate 3:06 into the first period on Nov. 1, 1959, at Madison Square Garden pierced Plante's face.

The blood escaped easily and quickly onto his jersey before pooling on the ice. The list of Plante's previous facial injuries was extensive: broken noses, a broken jaw and broken cheekbones totalling almost 200 stitches. He left the ice for repairs by the on-site doctor and the impact of the shot became apparent once Red Fisher, a legendary hockey journalist who spent 58 years covering the Canadiens for the Montreal *Star* and the Montreal *Gazette*, observed the scene in the arena's clinic.

"Plante was standing in front of the mirror and sort of separating the cut that ran from the corner of his mouth through his nostril and looking in the mirror," Fisher said. "He said to me, 'Pretty ugly, isn't it?' "

Approximately 20 minutes and a handful of stitches later, Plante was ready to return to the ice, but only if he could wear a colorless, fiberglass mask he'd begun using in practice three years before. Canadiens coach Toe Blake resisted the idea, but since teams weren't carrying backups at the time he eventually relented.

"Nobody in the whole wide world expected him to return to the ice wearing a mask," Fisher said.

Because he did, Plante revolutionized not only the position but the game forever.

He wasn't the first to don a mask. In 1930, Clint Benedict debuted a leather half-mask, but used it only briefly. Plante was the first to wear full-face protection and stick with it. The Canadiens beat the Rangers 3-1 to maintain what became an 18-game unbeaten streak. The season ended with a Stanley Cup. Other goalies began to adopt the mask as part of their gear until it became normal protocol. Plante was a renegade among traditionalists, a colorful character who studied the game and prodded its progress as a result. It's completely appropriate that he spearheaded a movement as vital and meaningful as this one.

"He was that kind of guy," Fisher said. "He was special."

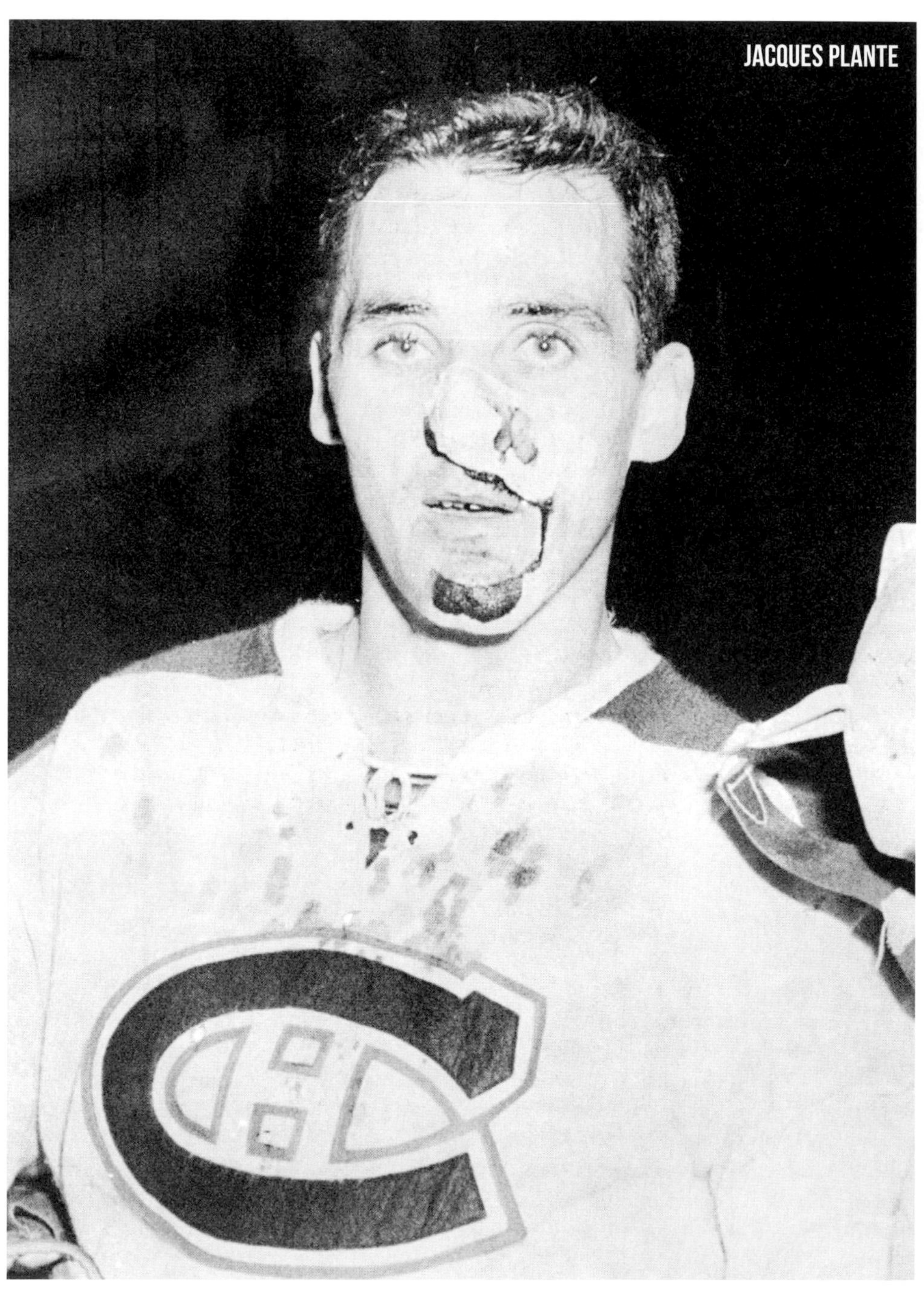
JACQUES PLANTE

THE CONTENDERS

KIRK MCLEAN

Considered one of the best saves in NHL history is McLean's sliding pad save on Robert Reichel in overtime during Game 7 in the 1994 Western Conference quarterfinal. Reichel was the beneficiary of what started as a 3-on-1 attack, firing a one-timer into what appeared to be a yawning cage before McLean kicked out his right pad to keep the Canucks alive against the favored Flames. Vancouver defeated Calgary in double overtime and eventually advanced to the Stanley Cup final.

FRANK PIETRANGELO

Known simply as 'The Save.' Pittsburgh Penguins backup Pietrangelo sprawled to make a glove save on New Jersey Devils center Peter Stastny in the first period of Game 6 in the Patrick Division semifinal in 1991. Pietrangelo's snag staved off elimination for the Penguins, who went on to win their first Cup.

MARC-ANDRE FLEURY

Fleury's Stanley Cup-saving stop on Nicklas Lidstrom in Game 7 of the 2009 final remains one of the most dramatic and clutch saves of all-time. In the dying seconds of the game, with Detroit down 2-1 to Pittsburgh, Lidstrom was looking at a wide-open net when Fleury deflected the puck straight to him after making a right pad save on Henrik Zetterberg. As Lidstrom charged toward the loose puck at the lower left circle, Fleury scrambled to his right and threw his body headfirst to make the stop with two seconds left. The save gave the Penguins their third title in franchise history and stopped the Red Wings' run at a second straight championship.

CHAPTER 32

BIGGEST GOALIE PADS

GARTH SNOW

BY MATT LARKIN

THE DEAD PUCK ERA featured some legendary goaltenders in their primes: Patrick Roy, Dominik Hasek, Martin Brodeur and Ed Belfour, among others. And though there's no denying the brilliance of that quartet, their numbers also sparkle because they come from a time in which the neutral zone trap shrunk scoring significantly and goalies had no limit on their equipment size.

If you don't believe goalies had it made in the armor department during the late 1990s and early 2000s, Google "Michelin Man" and "NHL goalie." Chances are you'll get plenty of hits with a specific name: Garth Snow.

Compared by many to baseball's Gaylord Perry, Snow is the unofficial granddaddy of goalie equipment that cheated without cheating. The journeyman goaltender came under the microscope in the Philadelphia Flyers' run to the Stanley Cup final in 1997. He stood tall and wide in the Philly net thanks to the oversized lacrosse-style pads he wore. After opponents cried foul, the NHL outlawed Snow's torso armor in time for the following season.

But Snow wasn't done trying to beat the system. For several seasons afterward, he used extremely tall goalie pads. The NHL's lone restriction at the time was that pads not exceed 12 inches in width. However, netminders could make them as tall as they wanted. Snow deployed thigh-highs, which came almost all the way to his waist. At first glance, they simply looked like smart protection for a 6-foot-3 goaltender. When Snow dropped into a butterfly, however, the tips of his pads completely covered his five-hole.

The league had had enough by 2003 and installed a rule limiting goalie pad height to 38 inches. Snow publicly objected at the time, but years later he spoke out in favor of reducing equipment size. His pads were reported to be as tall as 43 inches – three-and-a-half feet – before the crackdown.

“ WHEN HE DROPPED INTO A BUTTERFLY, THE TIPS OF HIS PADS COMPLETELY COVERED HIS FIVE-HOLE ”

BIGGEST GOALIE PADS

GARTH SNOW

THE CONTENDERS

PATRICK ROY

'Saint Patrick' wasn't just an innovator in that he popularized the butterfly style. He was also quite the experimenter with his equipment. He tried out various oversized pieces and notoriously wore tablecloth-like jerseys intended to trap loose pucks. Roy even colored the five-hole on his pads white to trick shooters into thinking they had open looks.

JEAN-SEBASTIEN GIGUERE

The playoff hero goaltender had his pads scrutinized at various stages of his career, most notably during his Conn Smythe performance with the Anaheim Ducks in the 2003 playoffs when Claude Lemieux of the Dallas Stars called him out publicly. Various teams filed complaints the following fall, claiming Giguere's pads were illegal.

MIKE DUNHAM

The NHL slapped Dunham on the (padded) wrist at the same time it went after Snow, ordering him to reduce his pad size. He lamented the discipline in the press, worrying that he'd be injured as a result of smaller equipment.

CHAPTER 33

BIGGEST BLOWOUT

DETROIT RED WINGS 15, NEW YORK RANGERS 0

BY BOB DUFF

FOR A MAN THOUGHT by many as the greatest all-around athlete to come out of Edmonton, Ken McAuley is remembered more for what was likely the worst night of his athletic career. McAuley was a top-notch goaltender who earned a spot with the New York Rangers in 1943. He also starred in fastball, baseball, soccer and lacrosse and he was the all-star quarterback in the Edmonton Junior Football League in 1941. It was his work between the pipes, however, that earned McAuley his place in hockey humiliation.

The outbreak of the Second World War devastated NHL rosters as young stars hurried to enlist and aid the war effort. The Rangers roster was gutted as players joined the military, but there was one bright spot as the team broke camp for the start of 1943-44.

"The Blueshirts are said to have uncovered a fine goalie in Ken McAuley, formerly of Edmonton," reported the Montreal *Gazette* on the eve of the regular season.

Unfortunately for McAuley, little else was fine for the Rangers, who finished last in 1942-43. New York opened '43-44 with 11 straight losses. In single games over the course of the season, Chicago put 10 goals past McAuley, Toronto pounded 11 behind him and Boston lit him up 13 times.

"It's to the credit of McAuley's upbringing that he does not kick little children into the gutter on his daily constitutional along Eighth Avenue," read the New York *World-Telegram*. "His only rest is during intermissions. He should be paid time and a half for most games."

McAuley, who worked as a probation officer in Edmonton prior to turning pro, didn't get paroled from long nights in net. The worst came on Jan. 23, 1944, when the Rangers visited Olympia Stadium to tangle with Detroit. Led by a hat trick from veteran Syd Howe, the Red Wings blitzkrieged McAuley and the Rangers 15-0 – the most lopsided shutout in NHL history.

McAuley did his utmost to stem the tide, making 43 saves, but fatigue eventually got the better of him in the final frame. Detroit scored eight times during the period.

"They never even had to clear the other end of the ice," McAuley said. "It wasn't even marked."

The Wings got two goals each from Murray Armstrong, Don Grosso and Carl Liscombe.

Hal Jackson, Mud Bruneteau, Flash Hollett, Bill Quackenbush, Ken Kilrea and Adam Brown had one each. Every player figured in the scoring except goalie Connie Dion and defenseman Cully Simon.

Howe's hat trick came in the final period, giving him 149 career goals, one more than Herbie Lewis, making Howe Detroit's all-time goal-scoring leader. It was just one of eight marks established by the Wings during their record-setting performance. The final score remains the NHL's largest shutout and the 15-goal difference the biggest margin of victory ever recorded. The streak of 15 consecutive goals scored in one game is also still on the books. Other records set that night that have since fallen include most points for one team in one game (37), and most goals (eight) and most points (22) by a team in one period.

At the game's conclusion, the beleaguered McAuley stormed into the Rangers dressing room, slammed his stick to the floor and refused to speak to his teammates. Defenseman Bucko McDonald, one of the team's few veterans, sought to calm the waters.

“THEY NEVER EVEN HAD TO CLEAR THE OTHER END OF THE ICE. IT WASN'T EVEN MARKED”

“Hey, don't let it worry you,” McDonald told McAuley. “There have been a lot of goalies in this league, but none of them ever set a record like that.”

McAuley just smiled and nodded.

Teammate Billy Warwick, McAuley's brother-in-law, brought him a keepsake from the night. Warwick grabbed the goal light from behind the net McAuley had defended for two of the three periods and presented it to his goalie.

McAuley, who died in 1992, eventually learned to laugh about being the victim of the NHL's most lopsided loss.

“I ask people when they remind me of that night, ‘Where would the Detroit Red Wings have been without me?’ ” McAuley said later. “I gave them the confidence to become big stars.”

KEN McAULEY

THE CONTENDERS

MONTREAL CANADIENS 16, QUEBEC BULLDOGS 3 (MARCH 3, 1920)

Taking advantage of Quebec goalie Frank Brophy, who was slowed by a strained thigh ligament, Montreal poured in a record tally that has never been equalled. Newsy Lalonde scored four times, as did Harry Cameron, tying his own single-game record for defensemen. Didier Pitre and Odie Cleghorn each had three goals.

BUFFALO SABRES 14, TORONTO MAPLE LEAFS 4 (MARCH 19, 1981)

Leading 1-0 after one period, the Sabres exploded for an NHL-record nine-goal second period. The combined 12 goals in the period are also a league mark and Buffalo's 23 points in the frame tied an NHL record. Gilbert Perreault netted three goals in the second.

TORONTO MAPLE LEAFS 14, NEW YORK RANGERS 1 (MARCH 16, 1957)

Toronto, which came into the match as the NHL's lowest-scoring team, set a club record for goals in a game. Every Maple Leaf, except goalie Ed Chadwick and defenseman Jim Thomson, had a point, with Sid Smith and Brian Cullen getting hat tricks.

GILBERT PERREAULT

CHAPTER 34

BIGGEST COMEBACK

1941-42 TORONTO MAPLE LEAFS

BY STAN FISCHLER

IT NEVER HAPPENED BEFORE, nor has it happened since. And it very likely will never happen again.

Coached by Clarence 'Hap' Day, the 1941-42 Toronto Maple Leafs remain the only team to overcome a 3-0 deficit in the Stanley Cup final. They accomplished that feat because Day went totally against the coaching grain, and then some.

With his Maple Leafs on the cusp of elimination, Day benched Gordie Drillon, his leading goal scorer, as well as his top defenseman, Bucko McDonald. Drillon was replaced by a mostly minor league grunt, Don Metz, kid brother of Toronto forward Nick Metz. McDonald's stand-in was an inexperienced rookie, Ernie Dickens, backed by another freshman, Bob Goldham.

Based on those nutsy moves, the 13,694 fans that jammed Olympia Stadium on April 12, 1942, had good reason to believe their Detroit Red Wings would soon celebrate their third Stanley Cup. Wally Stanowski, a third-year defenseman on the Leafs, remembers the arrogance of Detroit's boss, coach-GM Jack Adams, who had already predicted the win.

"Adams went on the radio and said his club was ready to wrap up the series," Stanowski said. "That fired us up as much as anything."

Prior to the fateful game, Day read a letter to his troops from a 14-year-old Toronto girl who still believed in her Leafs. When Day finished, Sweeney Schriner leaped off his bench and said, "Don't worry, Skipper, we'll win this one for the little girl."

And so they did, 4-3, after which an irate Adams leaped onto the ice after the final buzzer and pummelled referee Mel Harwood until officials and police intervened. After viewing the mayhem, NHL president Frank Calder suspended Adams indefinitely.

Meanwhile, Day kept rolling the dice. For Game 5 at Maple Leaf Gardens, he benched three-year vet Hank Goldup for 19-year-old left winger Gaye Stewart, even though the rookie was less than a year out of junior hockey. Don Metz mesmerized Red Wings goalie Johnny Mowers with a hat trick plus an assist. Stanowski assisted on Nick Metz's first goal, scored the second and set up Don Metz's third goal in the 9-3 rout.

Now the series was getting serious. In Game 6 at Olympia, Leafs goalie Turk Broda managed to preserve a 0-0 tie after the first period. With less than 15 seconds gone in the

CLARENCE 'HAP' DAY

" ADAMS WENT ON THE RADIO AND SAID HIS CLUB WAS READY TO WRAP UP THE SERIES. THAT FIRED US UP AS MUCH AS ANYTHING "

middle period, Don Metz (who else?) buried the puck behind Mowers for what proved to be the winning goal. Late in the final frame, rookies Goldham and Billy Taylor cushioned the lead, ensuring Broda's 3-0 blanking. Near the end, a Detroit fan summed up the prevailing opinion by hurling a dead fish on the ice.

"That fish," wrote Toronto author and former Leafs publicist Ed Fitkin, "was symbolic of Red Wings fans' reaction to the collapse of their team."

Tied 3-3, the series was up for grabs in the decisive Game 7 on April 18, 1942. With the Second World War underway, players on both sides realized they would soon enlist in the armed forces. For many, this would be their last game until they returned. Some, such as Leafs boss Conn Smythe, were already in khaki. 'The Little Major' was granted leave from his base in Petawawa, Ont. That explains why the uniformed Smythe was one of the 16,218 spectators, the largest crowd in NHL history up to that point, in the rink he'd helped build a decade earlier.

After two periods, no miracle appeared to be at hand. Detroit led 1-0 and Smythe, who earlier had vowed to stay away from the Toronto dressing room, changed his mind because he had a brainstorm.

"I could see that the game had slowed down," Smythe wrote in his autobiography, *If You Can't Beat 'Em in the Alley*. "That made the game exactly right for old Sweeney Schriner, old Lorne Carr and young Billy Taylor and I told them."

Sure enough, with the Wings shorthanded in the third period, Day heeded Smythe's advice and deployed Schriner, Carr and Taylor on the power play. Once again the roulette ball fell into the Leafs' slot. Carr and Taylor crafted passes that eventually sent the puck to Schriner, who beat Mowers at 7:46. After the roars had finally subsided, Day gambled again, dispatching veteran Bob Davidson with youngsters Pete Langelle, Johnny McCreedy and Goldham. Youth would be served when McCreedy penetrated the Detroit blueline and fired the rubber at Mowers. The Wings goalie stopped the shot, but his rebound skimmed tantalizingly to Langelle, who deposited it for the go-ahead goal. Minutes later Schriner proved Smythe a genius by delivering the insurance marker.

The bulging Maple Leaf Gardens rocked as never before with all eyes on the overhead clock. As the final seconds wound down, the fans helped it along: "...three, two, one..." Fitkin described the scene: "Pandemonium broke loose on the ice and in the stands. The crowd roared with the ecstasy of the moment."

And why not? The Leafs had manufactured a miracle and no Cup finalist has created one like it ever since.

THE CONTENDERS

PHILADELPHIA FLYERS VS. BOSTON BRUINS

In the second round of the 2010 playoffs, Philadelphia stared at a 0-3 deficit against Boston. How was the insurmountable surmounted? It began with Simon Gagne's Game 4 overtime goal. The revitalized Flyers then took Game 5, 4-0, and Mike Richards paced the home club to a 2-1 triumph in Game 6, tying the series.

The series now shifted to Beantown for Game 7. Before the first period had ended, however, Philadelphia was down 3-0 to Boston. But the Flyers rebounded again when James van Riemsdyk beat goalie Tuukka Rask. In the second, goals by Scott Hartnell and Danny Briere made it 3-3. The tie held until 11:10 in the third period, when the Bruins were penalized for having too many men on the ice. Gagne delivered again with the winning goal and Flyers fans celebrated the most remarkable comeback of the young millennium.

NEW YORK ISLANDERS VS. PITTSBURGH PENGUINS

Having squeezed into a playoff berth for the first time in franchise history, the Islanders opened the 1975 post-season with a series victory over the heavily favored Rangers. Thrust into the second round against Pittsburgh, the Nassaumen dropped the first three games and appeared doomed to be ousted in Game 4. Coach Al Arbour replaced goalie Billy Smith with Glenn 'Chico' Resch and the gambit paid off in a 3-1 victory. The teams returned to Steeltown for Game 5, where Resch backstopped the Islanders to a 4-2 triumph, followed by a 4-1 win at home.

Back at the Igloo, with the series tied, the teams were deadlocked 0-0 until 14:42 in the third period when Islanders captain Ed Westfall took a pass from defenseman Bert Marshall and fired the puck behind the Penguins' Gary Inness. The home club never could foil Resch and the improbable upset ended with Islanders on top, 1-0.

WILKES-BARRE/SCRANTON PENGUINS VS. PROVIDENCE BRUINS

In the second round of the 2013 American League playoffs, Wilkes-Barre/Scranton trailed by three games, but fought back to capture the series. Leading the comeback up front were Trevor Smith and Chad Kolarik, while Brian Dumoulin paced the back end and Brad Thiessen got hot in net.

Providence finished first overall in the regular season, but problems with its NHL parent club in Boston led to its collapse. With three defensemen injured, the big B's dipped into their AHL affiliate. One of those blueliners was Matt Bartkowski, Providence's best defenseman at the time. Another good one was Torey Krug. Their absence spurred one of the most classic collapses in AHL annals.

SIMON GAGNE

CHAPTER 35

BIGGEST UPSET

1981-82 LOS ANGELES KINGS

BY KEN CAMPBELL

HISTORY HAS TOLD US time and again that the Edmonton Oilers truly became a championship team after being swept by the New York Islanders in the 1983 Stanley Cup final. As they walked past the Islanders' dressing room, they saw more players tending to battle wounds than celebrating their fourth straight championship.

Now, Daryl Evans has never studied history, but he figures a lot of the credit for the molding of the Oilers' 1980s dynasty should go to the Los Angeles Kings from the season prior. That's because those Kings taught the Oilers a potent lesson in underestimating an opponent. Which is why Los Angeles' triumph over Edmonton that spring is considered the most unlikely upset in NHL history.

To be sure, the best-of-five Smythe Division semifinal between the Kings and Oilers in 1982 couldn't have been more of a mismatch on paper if it were the Washington Generals taking on the Harlem Globetrotters. The young, run-and-gun Oilers were cutting a swath through the NHL, scoring goals by the bushel and serving notice that they were a legitimate Stanley Cup contender. In their eight games against Los Angeles that season, Edmonton won five games (two by a touchdown), lost only once and tied the other two, outscoring the Kings 51-27. Led by 200-point man Wayne Gretzky, the Oilers scored 417 goals, becoming the first team in NHL history to score 400 goals in a season.

"I don't think we scored 400 that season," said Evans, now a radio analyst with Los Angeles, "even if you counted all the goals we scored in practice."

"I DON'T THINK WE SCORED 400 THAT SEASON, EVEN IF YOU COUNTED ALL THE GOALS WE SCORED IN PRACTICE"

MARCEL DIONNE

Not only had the Kings finished a whopping 48 points behind the Oilers in the Smythe Division, they were a team in disarray. Their 63 points were the worst among the 16 teams that had qualified for the playoffs and they'd won just one of their final eight games. The only reason they made the playoffs was that they were in the same division as the woeful Colorado Rockies, who moved to New Jersey after the season. Los Angeles coach Parker MacDonald was fired after getting off to a 13-24-5 start, but things weren't much better under Don Perry, who went 11-17-10.

And the Kings weren't exactly a playoff juggernaut. Prior to that season, they had won three playoff series in their 14-year existence and had been ousted in the preliminary round of the playoffs in each of the previous four seasons. Los Angeles was full marks for its reputation as a playoff failure, but the team had also been invigorated by some good young talent to support their superstar Marcel Dionne. Future Hall of Famer Larry Murphy was one season removed from establishing an NHL record for points by a rookie defenseman. Bernie Nicholls had come up from the minors and scored 32 points in 22 games and Evans gave the Kings some much-needed youthful energy.

"We really had no business being there and we had nothing to lose," Evans said. "It was just, 'Go out and play and have fun,' and that's what we did. And I really think it was us young guys – like Steve Bozek and myself and Bernie Nicholls and Doug Smith – who energized the old guys, because we had all just finished playing junior hockey and we were used to crazy games where you're scoring goals all the time."

When faced with a mismatch of those proportions, most coaches of the underdog would likely implement a game plan that would see their team check the daylights out of the opponents and hope for a break or two on offense. Perry, however, took the opposite approach. He figured the only way the Kings were going to beat the Oilers was to match them goal for goal and he was right.

Starting with the opening game of the series, in which Los Angeles was down 4-1 to Edmonton in the first period and came back to win 10-8, the Kings won all the high-scoring games in the series. Their other two wins were by 6-5 in overtime in the game famously dubbed the 'Miracle on Manchester' and 7-4 in the deciding game. Edmonton's two wins, one of which came in overtime, were both by a score of 3-2.

The thing that makes the 1982 Kings-Oilers series so unbelievable is it provided an upset within an upset. After Los Angeles had split the first two games of the series, the team came home to the Forum and looked awful in the first two periods, falling behind 5-0. Owner Jerry Buss left the game after the second to beat the traffic on the way home and Gretzky and the Oilers were laughing at the Kings. Los Angeles retreated to the dressing room hoping to win the third period and get a good feeling going heading into Game 4.

"Even at that point if someone had said, 'After three games, you're only going to be trailing 2-1 and not out of the series,' we probably would have said, 'OK, sign us up. We'll take that,' " Evans said.

Starting with a tally by Jay Wells 2:46 into the third, the goals kept coming. With six minutes left in the game, it was still 5-2 for the Oilers, but the Kings poured it on, scoring

> **“WE REALLY HAD NO BUSINESS BEING THERE AND WE HAD NOTHING TO LOSE. IT WAS JUST, ‘GO OUT AND PLAY AND HAVE FUN,’ AND THAT’S WHAT WE DID”**

three more times, including the game-tying goal with their goalie pulled with five seconds left in the period. And when Evans scored at 2:35 of overtime to cap the comeback, the home crowd erupted. It’s still remembered as one of the greatest moments in the history of sports in Los Angeles.

The Kings lost Game 4 and then went on to win the series in Game 5 in Edmonton, capping the greatest upset ever. They didn’t do much more after that, however, losing to the Vancouver Canucks in five games in the next round and then missing the playoffs in three of the next four seasons. But nothing will overshadow the win over the Oilers in 1982, the Miracle on Manchester and the team that took the swagger away from the Oilers, at least for a little while.

“I probably appreciate it more now than I actually did at the time,” Evans said. “This league has been around about 100 years and nobody has ever seen anything like that.”

THE CONTENDERS

U.S. OVER U.S.S.R.

Not much was expected of the 1980 United States Olympic team going into the Winter Olympics, but it quickly became a team of destiny. By the time the Americans faced the powerful Soviets in the semifinals, a gold medal was within reach. But even then, nobody expected a bunch of college kids and minor leaguers to actually challenge what was arguably the best team in the world, particularly after the Americans were crushed 10-3 by the Soviets at Madison Square Garden just prior to the Games.

Thanks to standout goaltending from Jim Craig, the U.S. was down just 3-2 heading into the third period. The Americans scored twice in the final frame to take a 4-3 lead, prompting broadcaster Al Michaels to utter the famous sentence: "Do you believe in miracles? Yes!" The U.S. defeated Finland two days later to win the gold medal.

CHICAGO OVER TORONTO

In 1937-38, Chicago limped down the stretch, losing its last three games of the season by a combined score of 13-3, finishing just two points ahead of the Detroit Red Wings in the American Division with a record of 14-25-9. After stunning the Montreal Canadiens and New York Americans in the first two rounds of the playoffs, the Black Hawks found themselves in the Stanley Cup final against the star-studded Toronto Maple Leafs. With goalie Mike Karakas hurt, the Hawks used the Maple Leafs' spare goaltender and won the first game of the series before going on to win the series 3-1. It remains one of the biggest upsets in NHL history and marks the Hawks as the worst statistical team to ever win the Cup.

BELARUS OVER SWEDEN

Despite being a million-to-one long shot to win the gold medal in the 2002 Winter Olympics, Belarus somehow found itself in the quarterfinal against Sweden in what was supposed to be a rout. But the Swedes played with absolutely no urgency and found themselves in a 3-3 tie in the third period. Then Vladimir Kopat took a long slapshot that bounced off the head of Sweden's goalie Tommy Salo and into the net, giving Belarus its own Miracle on Ice and Sweden its biggest hockey debacle. The day after the game, one Swedish newspaper published each player's picture on the front page, along with his NHL salary and the word "Traitor."

BIGGEST UPSET

BELARUS BEATS SWEDEN

CHAPTER 36

BIGGEST MELTDOWN

2012-13 TORONTO MAPLE LEAFS

BY MATT LARKIN

"It was just a perfect, colossal, unfortunate event."
– James Reimer

OH, THE HUMILIATION. NO team in NHL history had ever blown a three-goal lead in the third period of a Game 7 until the 2012-13 Toronto Maple Leafs came along. In doing so, they added one more deep, gnarly scar to a long-abused fan base.

"I didn't talk to anyone after the game," said goaltender James Reimer. "It was a pretty tough one. That night I didn't fall asleep until about 7:30 in the morning, just lying there thinking about it."

It was the perfect storm, largely because it began as a story of real triumph.

This was the Toronto team that had broken a curse. In an entire era – 2005-06 to 2011-12, lockout to lockout – the Maple Leafs were the sole franchise not to make the playoffs. Things were different in 2012-13. New coach Randy Carlyle re-energized Toronto, as did breakout youngster Nazem Kadri. The Leafs hit and fought more than any other team in the league and finally returned to the post-season with a new persona.

Of all the opponents, however, Toronto had to draw Boston, its own private bogeyman. No matter how you broke down the series, the Bruins had the Maple Leafs' number. Boston had the mental edge because a couple lopsided trades with Toronto over the years netted it franchise cornerstones in starting goalie Tuukka Rask, sniper Tyler Seguin (later dealt to the Dallas Stars after the 2013 playoffs) and rookie defenseman Dougie Hamilton. The Leafs got elite goal scorer Phil Kessel out of one of the deals, but little else. And he couldn't visit Boston without endless ridicule and "Thank you, Kessel!" chants echoing throughout TD Garden.

The numbers suggested the young, inexperienced Leafs were in huge trouble. Kessel had three goals and was a minus-22 in 22 games against his old team entering the series. Boston was 25-6-6 in its previous 37 games against Toronto. It was set up to be a romp.

Through four games, the series was going just that way. Playoff dynamo David Krejci had just broken Toronto's heart with an overtime winner at the Air Canada Centre, giving the Bruins a 3-1 series lead heading back to Boston. The series was as good as over.

Then something happened. The Leafs grew up. They pushed back, even Kessel. And they had Boston on the brink of elimination. Or so everyone thought.

Reimer stood on his head in Game 5 in an improbable 2-1 victory. The Leafs took Game 6 at home with an inspired effort, including a game-winner from Kessel, and forced a deciding game.

In that Game 7, Toronto began doing the unthinkable. It began slaying the dragon. The team withstood an initial onslaught to tie the contest 1-1 after one period. Defenseman Cody Franson added a second consecutive goal to give Toronto a 2-1 edge entering the third. And when the final stanza started, the young, green Leafs didn't wilt. Kessel and Kadri each fired a puck past Rask. Leafs Nation rejoiced.

Nearly halfway through the period, it was still a 4-1 game. Thousands of crushed Bruins fans filed out of TD Garden. The Leafs could barely contain their grins on the bench. The demon was being exorcised.

> **"THAT'S IT, YOUR SEASON'S DONE. THERE'S NOT TOMORROW, THERE'S NOT THE NEXT DAY, THERE'S NOT 'GET 'EM NEXT TIME.' IT'S JUST DONE. IT'S AN EMPTY FEELING"**

Cue the most stunning, improbable Game 7 comeback in NHL history. In theory, it didn't matter how well Boston could play in the final 11 minutes. This wasn't the 1980s and even an all-star team had trouble scoring three times in 11 minutes in this era. The Bruins could dominate the play and simply not have time to come back. Everything had to go perfectly for it to happen. And it did.

"We thought we were doing some good things, getting the puck out, just trying to obviously hold onto the lead," said Leafs left winger James van Riemsdyk. "And maybe that's where it went wrong. Maybe we could have tried to hem them in a little more, play some more time in their zone. But they're a good team and they were coming hard with some speed and they definitely weren't going to go away easy."

When Nathan Horton beat Reimer to make it 4-2 with 10-plus minutes remaining in the third, no one really batted an eyelash. It was an extra tally to make the final score respectable, nothing more. The Bruins' body language wasn't particularly perky. A lot of people forget it already, but nine whole minutes passed before Boston scored again.

The Leafs were leading 4-2 with 1:22 to play. Then came the goal that turned the tide.

37

BOYCHUK
55
GARDINER
51

“THAT HOCKEY GAME WILL HAUNT ME UNTIL THE DAY I DIE...”

Reimer couldn’t control a Zdeno Chara point shot and a juicy rebound squirted onto Milan Lucic’s stick. He buried it and immediately rallied the troops, telling them all, “One more!” The big bad Bruins’ bench swelled.

If Toronto had realized the best defense was a strong offense, that pinning Boston in its own territory wasn’t a silly gamble but a necessary measure to keep its own goal safe, the comeback would have ended there. Yet the Leafs turned into terrified children, hiding under the bed from the bogeyman. They chipped the puck out and into Boston’s possession as soon as they crossed the red line. The Bruins were relentless, peppering Reimer with 17 shots in the third period. The equalizer came with 51 seconds left in regulation when Chara, all 6-foot-9 of him, screened Reimer on a Patrice Bergeron wrist shot.

“I remember looking and trying to see the puck,” Reimer said. “Couldn’t see it. But I could see his (Bergeron’s) body, that he was shooting, from his shoulders. I just tried to go down and be as big as I could. And I felt it graze my shoulder. It’s a bad feeling because I knew it didn’t hit me enough for it to go wide. I knew it was going in. It was tough. There are not really words.”

One look at the Leafs bench after that goal told you the game was all but over. Cameras panned across a sea of wide-eyed, stunned faces. It was almost as if they knew they’d lose the overtime. Although Joffrey Lupul had a quality scoring chance in the extra frame, the Leafs indeed lost and it was Bergeron twisting the dagger again, shooting the puck into an open cage when the Leafs couldn’t clear on a mad scramble in front of Reimer.

“All of a sudden the puck just went flying over there, right on his tape,” Reimer said. “And that’s it, your season’s done. There’s not tomorrow, there’s not the next day, there’s not, ‘Get ’em next time.’ It’s just done. It’s an empty feeling.”

There is nothing quite like the empty feeling of being a Leafs fan in the post-expansion era. Being one requires supporting a team that hasn’t won a Stanley Cup in almost 50 years and last triumphed in the final season of the pre-expansion era. In other words, the Leafs last won it all the last year it was ‘easy.’

To cheer for the Leafs is to celebrate near misses as successes, to give Doug Gilmour and Mats Sundin standing ovations and reminisce on storied trips to the conference final. That’s right, the semifinal. Toronto hasn’t even reached the final since 1967.

To bleed Blue and White also means lamenting a series of devastating defeats over the years. Wayne Gretzky stole glory from the Leafs in Game 6 of the 1993 Western Conference final when his high-stick on Gilmour went unnoticed by referee Kerry Fraser, whose villainy in Hogtown was immortalized that day. In 2002, after Sundin tied Game 6 of the Eastern Conference final against the Carolina Hurricanes with 22 seconds left, Martin

Gelinas broke Leafs Nation's heart eight minutes into overtime. Then there was the 2007 debacle in which a mere mediocre shootout performance from journeyman New York Islanders goalie Wade Dubielewicz would have punched Toronto's ticket to the playoffs on the final day of the regular season. Instead, he stood on his head and led the Islanders past the New Jersey Devils.

Perhaps only a long-suffering franchise like MLB's Chicago Cubs can understand the scrutiny and humiliation the Leafs have suffered over the years. Like the Cubbies', Toronto's fan base is especially large, especially loyal and, at times, especially sad. Something about Leafs Nation has always drawn the ire of other fans. If you aren't a Leafs supporter, admit it: you love seeing them and their fans wallow in misery year after year. You point your finger at the hilarity.

Perhaps that's what made Toronto's meltdown in Game 7 of the Eastern Conference final especially cruel. The way it happened was embarrassing and unprecedented enough, but for the Leafs, of all teams, to suffer it attracted the type of ridicule no other sad sack NHL franchise could have. Toronto had much to be proud of after a series in which it stood up to a schoolyard bully. In the end, however, the 2012-13 Leafs will forever be known as the club that choked like no other in post-season history, one that made the three-goal lead in the third period 'the most dangerous in hockey.' In the days that followed, the Blue and White endured a hangover like few others.

"Everyone's still in a bit of shock and disbelief," Kadri said. "At the same time, it's not like you can just go and hide in a dark hole for the next couple weeks and just try to forget about everything that happened. You've got to accept it and take the positives and move forward."

Kadri and some of his teammates may one day get over it. For others, however, it's a game that will never go away. Lupul is one such player. And he let Leafs Nation know his pain when he took to Twitter the day after the Leafs' historic meltdown.

"That hockey game will haunt me until the day I die..."

THE CONTENDERS

VANCOUVER RIOT

Although carnage followed the Canucks' on-ice failure, the fans, not the team, suffered the real meltdown on June 15, 2011. Vancouver had a chance to close out Boston on home ice in Game 7 of the Stanley Cup final for its first championship. Instead, the Canucks came out flat as a board and lost 4-0 to the Bruins. Devastated fans took to the streets and gave the city a permanent black mark. Over 100 were injured and hundreds more arrested and later charged as civilians battled the police, burning multiple cruisers. The downtown core became a sea of fire, tear gas and broken glass as furious fans caused millions of dollars in property damage.

THE CONTENDERS

DAVE HODGE

After a Toronto game ended early on CBC the evening of March 14, 1987, the network aired regional coverage of a Montreal Canadiens/Philadelphia Flyers tilt. It went to overtime, but when the clock struck 11:00 p.m., CBC abandoned the game for the news. Hodge, the *Hockey Night in Canada* anchor, was disgusted and shared his feelings with the camera: "Now, Montreal and the Philadelphia Flyers are currently playing in overtime, and… we are not able to go there. That's the way things go today in sports and this network. And the Flyers and the Canadiens have us in suspense and we'll remain that way until we can find out somehow who won this game, or who's responsible for the way we do things here. Goodnight for *Hockey Night in Canada*." Hodge punctuated his speech by flipping his pen in the air. He was axed from the network within a week.

PATRICK LALIME

As Ottawa contended in the early 2000s, goaltender Patrick Lalime was known for posting solid numbers on paper, but failing the Senators in crucial moments. None was more defining than Game 7 of Ottawa's 2004 Eastern Conference quarterfinal matchup against Toronto on April 20, 2004. With the Leafs up 1-0 at home, Joe Nieuwendyk fluttered a harmless wrist shot toward Lalime from a bad angle outside the top of the circle along the boards. It somehow got through on the short side to put Toronto up 2-0. With 21 seconds left in the first period, Nieuwendyk let another wrister go from almost the same spot. It beat Lalime through the wickets. He collapsed in a humiliated heap. Coach Jacques Martin pulled him after three goals on 11 shots. Lalime was never the same, relegated to backup duty for the rest of his career.

CHAPTER 37

BIGGEST TOURNAMENT

1972 SUMMIT SERIES

BY SARAH McLELLAN

THE SIGNIFICANCE OF THE images, names and feelings surrounding the Summit Series in September 1972 only seems to deepen with time. They become more vivid and celebrated as they're handed down through the generations on a trajectory to eclipse past triumphs in the present consciousness. And yet when it was actually happening, the importance of the series wasn't immediately clear to the participants.

The eight-game battle was the first meeting between the Soviet national team and a Canadian contingent of NHL players and was hyped as a collision of the two premier hockey powers in the world. The Soviets had won gold at the three previous Winter Olympics and were ruling international competition, from which the Canadians excluded their best talent because the International Ice Hockey Federation and International Olympic Committee wouldn't admit professional players.

The event became a cultural phenomenon, a source of national pride and a transformative chapter in hockey's history. And all of it, all of the responsibility, glory and innovation, was lost on the players until they were immersed in the action.

"After that first game, we realized immediately that this was serious and we're going to have to do what we have to do to win," said Canadian center Phil Esposito. "And whatever it took, we had to do it. And that's the way we proceeded from there."

The series took place at the height of the Cold War, a prolonged state of political and military hostility between the United States and its allies, including Canada, and the Communist countries in Europe, led by the Soviet Union. Hockey was tasked with transcending the tension.

The 35-member Canadian team, which notably excluded Bobby Hull after he joined the burgeoning World Hockey Association, descended on Toronto for a three-week training camp. Bobby Orr tagged along, but couldn't play because of a recent surgery on one of his badly injured knees. Despite the Canadians' unfamiliarity with the Soviets' style of play, they were expected to sweep – so much so that anything less would have been a crushing disappointment. Yet the Canadians lost 7-3 in Game 1 in Montreal and shock swallowed the country.

"We were not in shape," Esposito said. "We weren't a team yet. We were a bunch of guys

BIGGEST TOURNAMENT

1972 SUMMIT SERIES

that played against each other all the time and you don't win unless you're a team. We had to get that together as quickly as possible and that was most difficult to do."

The second game, in Toronto, yielded better results for the Canadians, who won 4-1. Game 3 was a 4-4 tie. Then the Soviets pulled out a 5-3 win in Game 4 in Vancouver, the last match on Canadian soil, and the final horn was greeted with a chorus of boos from the home fans. Esposito, then at the peak of his career, delivered a passionate monologue on national TV. He asked why he and his teammates deserved such a reaction when they were trying so tirelessly to win and to win for their country, which was the reason they agreed to face the Soviets in the first place.

"We had nobody but ourselves," he said.

The Canadians travelled overseas and with a two-week gap before Game 5 they stopped in Sweden for a pair of exhibition games.

"That's when we solidified us being a team," Esposito said.

A change of scenery didn't immediately help the Canadians solve the problem of the talented Soviets, led by goalie Vladislav Tretiak, captain Boris Mikhailov and talented scorer Alexander Yakushev. They corralled a 5-4 win in Game 5 in Moscow to take a 3-1-1 series lead.

Now that Canada needed three wins to rally, the intensity and urgency skyrocketed. Bobby Clarke slashed Valeri Kharlamov across his left skate in a controversial sequence after being prompted by assistant coach John Ferguson, who told Clarke the Russian star "needs a tap on the ankle." The slash broke Kharlamov's ankle, causing him to miss Game 7 and rendering him ineffective for the remainder of the series. The Canadians took the sixth game 3-2. Esposito, who ended up leading the series in scoring with seven goals and six assists, scored twice en route to a 4-3 win in Game 7.

The comeback wasn't complete, however, until Game 8 on Sept. 28. And that was still a dogged challenge.

The Canadians trailed 5-3 after the second period, but the Soviets shelved the speed and skill and puck movement that had surprised the Canadians early in the series in favor of a defensive posture. And Canada pounced. Esposito trimmed the deficit to one and Yvan Cournoyer, a right winger with the Montreal Canadiens, tied it.

"We can't lose," Esposito said. "That's the way I looked at it."

Then, with 34 seconds left, Esposito's shot was turned away by Tretiak, but Paul Henderson scooped up the rebound. He made one attempt, and then a second, before the puck went in and Canada secured a 6-5 victory. Henderson's goal became iconic – in hockey, Canadian lore and the entire Cold War. It was dubbed "the goal heard 'round the world" and it bridged the gap that had separated the two titans of the sport.

In its wake, the Summit Series sparked a host of other Canada-Russia tournaments. But none of those competitions could ever match the significance of that first meeting. It's possible no tournament ever will.

"It was a fabulous series," Esposito said. "People loved it. People loved it."

THE CONTENDERS

1987 CANADA CUP

The Soviets were at the center of yet another monumental tournament: the 1987 Canada Cup. This was the only meaningful time Wayne Gretzky and Mario Lemieux united on a line and they dominated the competition in leading Canada to a 2-1 series victory in the final. In Game 3, Canada overcame a 3-0 deficit. Then, with the score tied 5-5 and 1:26 remaining, Gretzky set up Lemieux for the game-winner in one of the country's most celebrated goals.

1996 WORLD CUP

The inaugural World Cup was the year the United States became a legitimate international threat. Led by dual citizen, Brett Hull, who chose to play for the U.S., despite being born in Canada, the Yankees bounced the Canadians in the three-game series final and on enemy territory, no less. The Americans dropped Game 1 in Philadelphia, 4-3 overtime, but bounced back with consecutive 5-2 wins in Montreal to take the three-game series 2-1. Canada's newest and biggest rival was now right next door.

2002 WINTER OLYMPICS

The Salt Lake City Games were memorable for Canada because they produced its first gold medal in 50 years. In the gold medal game, the Canadians took on the rising hockey power of the host country, as the U.S. continued to show its emergence as an international force. Canada came out on top with a 5-2 win with Joe Sakic scoring the game-winner, capping a four-point game for him, to lead the way for the Canadians.

BIGGEST TOURNAMENT

2002 OLYMPICS

CHAPTER 38

BIGGEST RANT

WAYNE GRETZKY

BY ADAM PROTEAU

WAYNE GRETZKY'S FAMOUS RANT at the 2002 Winter Olympics in Salt Lake City, Utah, was approximately nine minutes long and began rather innocuously. Although The Great One, who was the architect of Team Canada, started his tirade looking calm and collected, by the time he left the microphones at the podium he'd put together an incredibly passionate, us-against-the-world defense of his players that some argue motivated them to win a men's hockey gold medal for Canada for the first time in a half-century.

Gretzky began the rant, which took place on Feb. 18, 2002, after a 3-3 tie against the Czech Republic, by referring to the pressure Canadian players were under. But he quickly began painting a picture of a team that was simply too nice to its opponents, far nicer than any other country acted toward Team Canada.

"I don't think we dislike those countries as much as they hate us," Gretzky said. "That's a fact. They don't like us. They want to see us fail. They love beating us. They might tell (reporters) something different. But believe me, when you're on the ice, that's what they say. They don't like us and we've got to get that same feeling towards them."

From there, Gretzky went full-blown patriot in a way Canadians aren't known for. Using a vicious cross-check on Theo Fleury by Czech defenseman Roman Hamrlik as a jumping-off point, Gretzky said he was nearly sickened by the aspersions cast on Team Canada and turned the focus in the other direction: if his players had done something similar, he said, they would have been derided for hooliganism. He laughed with a combination of amusement and disgust and said the opposition deserved not only a slew of penalties, but suspensions as well. He didn't throw chairs or kick over microphones, but he made it abundantly clear which side he was on.

"Am I hot?" Gretzky said. "Yeah, I'm hot. I'm tired of people taking shots at Canadian hockey."

When a reporter told Gretzky of reports that Canada's veteran players were unhappy with coach Pat Quinn's style, he called them "American propaganda." And he finished his press conference by reinforcing the notion that, despite all the adversity and legions of spectators who wanted to see them fail, the Canadian team was as resilient as any that had come before it.

"We've got a proud bunch in our locker room," Gretzky said. "I know the whole world

> **"AM I HOT? YEAH, I'M HOT. I'M TIRED OF PEOPLE TAKING SHOTS AT CANADIAN HOCKEY"**

wants us to lose, except for Canada and Canada fans and our players. And we'll be there. We'll be standing."

Sure enough, he was correct. Inspired by their leader's confidence, the Canadians shook off their sluggish start to the tournament and beat an upstart American team in the final. To this day, Gretzky denies the rant was staged. But its authenticity doesn't matter. The results do. And to that end, it couldn't have worked any better.

BRIAN BURKE

THE CONTENDERS

PHIL ESPOSITO

Esposito's famous TV tirade in Vancouver, which was conducted at ice level after he and his teammates lost Game 4 of the 1972 Summit Series against the Soviet Union, set the standard for all rants that followed. Esposito harshly dressed down Canadian fans for showering the team with boos while building up his fellow players as selfless patriots.

"All of us (players) are really disheartened and we're disillusioned and we're disappointed in some of the (fans)," he said. "I don't think it's fair that we should be booed."

Esposito's rant worked, as Canada came back to win the most emotional international series of all-time.

BRIAN BURKE

The former Canucks, Ducks and Maple Leafs GM is renowned for being one of the most colorful figures in hockey today and was at the peak of his rhetorical powers when he sharply criticized the officiating in Vancouver's 2002 playoff series against Detroit. Specifically, Burke thought the abuse the Canucks' young Swedes, Daniel and Henrik Sedin, were taking from the Red Wings wasn't being recognized by the referees.

"Sedin isn't Swedish for 'Punch me,'" Burke said, "or 'Headlock me in a scrum.'"

JOHN TORTORELLA

'Torts' is well known for his emotional media outbursts, but nobody was quite prepared when, in 2006 as coach of Tampa Bay, he sharply criticized goalie John Grahame for allowing four goals on 17 shots in the first two periods of the team's fourth playoff game against Ottawa.

"I'm getting tired of the 25-percent rule," Tortorella said. "It's deflating. We need the occasional save."

He didn't get it. The Lightning were eliminated by the Senators the next game.

CHAPTER 39

BIGGEST CROWD

MICHIGAN STADIUM

BY KYLE CICERELLA

RED BERENSON HAS DECADES of hockey memories, but none of his experiences is held in as high regard as when his Michigan Wolverines set the all-time record for spectators at a game.

In an event dubbed 'The Big Chill at the Big House,' the Wolverines hosted the rival Michigan State Spartans before 104,173 fans on Dec. 11, 2010, at Michigan Stadium in Ann Arbour. It wasn't the first time these two schools had played each other in an outdoor event (the Spartans had held a game in October 2001 at Spartan Stadium in East Lansing for 74,544 fans), but it was by far the biggest.

"I can never, ever forget that feeling of awesomeness that I had when I walked out to the rink as a coach," said Berenson, 73, who has coached the Wolverines since 1984. "The players were beside themselves. It was magical to have a crowd that big. We were just... in wow."

In preparation for setting up the rink, Michigan staff and co-ordinators studied other outdoor games. When they decided to push for a new attendance record, they knew the rivalry between the two schools, separated by only 60 miles, would draw the biggest crowd possible.

"It's college hockey, a chance for a record, a game against rival Michigan State, but it's an outdoor game and they have a special attraction," Berenson said. "It's been a back-and-forth rivalry, but these outdoor games – you forget about who's in first place. It's only about the rivalry and it brings out the best in both programs."

With any outdoor event, weather can play a factor. And unlike in 2001, when the Spartans hosted the Wolverines in October, a December date had more risk attached. A winter blizzard was called for, but the storm stayed away long enough for the fans to become part of history. Players kept heaters on the bench just in case the temperature dropped too low, though they were never needed.

"Here we are in December at Michigan Stadium and we got a perfect day," Berenson said. "It was cool and the ice was fast, players were flying, it was perfect. The next day they had a blizzard and the game would have been affected."

The crowd witnessed a 5-0 victory for Berenson and the Wolverines that day. There

BIGGEST CROWD

> **“I CAN NEVER, EVER FORGET THAT FEELING OF AWESOMENESS THAT I HAD WHEN I WALKED OUT TO THE RINK AS A COACH. THE PLAYERS WERE BESIDE THEMSELVES. IT WAS MAGICAL TO HAVE A CROWD THAT BIG. WE WERE JUST...IN WOW”**

was more to the experience in the stadium, however, than any game the schools had ever played before, which is why it is so memorable for a man who has 17 seasons of NHL experience and the 1972 Summit Series to compare it to.

“The celebration after each goal with fireworks was awesome, but just before they dropped the puck a stealth bomber came over and it was unbelievable,” Berenson said. “I’ve never seen anything like it. You never heard a thing until it was just about past. It came down low and swooped over the stadium.”

Carl Hagelin and Jon Merrill scored twice to lead Michigan offensively, but it was backup goalie Shawn Hunwick who stole the spotlight after being thrown into the game at the last minute and pitching a 34-save shutout. Adam Janecyk was supposed to get his regular start, but went down with a groin injury in the warmup and couldn’t play. Hunwick played the rest of the season and almost took the Wolverines to the national championship.

When the final horn sounded, Michigan celebrated its victory on the ice. Michigan State, which wasn’t in a rush to leave the ice as the loser, stuck around, too. A post-game celebration included fireworks into the sky from ice level and the top of the stadium while the Wolverines’ school band played in the background.

“Both teams stayed in the stadium and lingered,” Berenson said. “All the fans stayed. No one wanted to leave because it was so magical.”

BIGGEST CROWD

PITTSBURGH vs. BUFFALO

THE CONTENDERS

PITTSBURGH PENGUINS VS. BUFFALO SABRES

To set the NHL record for attendance, the game needed to be taken out of the arena. So on Jan. 1, 2008, 71,217 fans packed Ralph Wilson Stadium in Orchard Park, N.Y., to see Buffalo host Pittsburgh in the NHL's first Winter Classic. Sidney Crosby scored the winner in the shootout and was named the game's first star. Ty Conklin made 36 saves for a 2-1 win. The NHL plans to set a new record for an outdoor game in 2014 with Detroit hosting Toronto at Michigan Stadium.

PHILADELPHIA FLYERS VS. TAMPA BAY LIGHTNING

The largest attendance for an indoor NHL game occurred in the playoffs when Tampa Bay hosted Philadelphia at Tropicana Field in St. Petersburg, Fla. The stadium, which was once designed for hockey and called the Thunderdome, had 28,183 people show up to watch Game 4 of the Eastern Conference quarterfinal on April 23, 1996. The Lightning were in the post-season for the first time in their short history and held a 2-1 series lead before dropping Game 4 to the Flyers in front of the record-setting crowd.

UNITED STATES VS. GERMANY

It was extra special for Germany when it beat Team USA on May 7, 2010, but not simply because it was the country's first win against the Americans in nearly two decades. Veltins-Arena was built for soccer in the city of Gelsenkirchen, Germany, but it was converted for the opening game of the 74th World Championship and an international record crowd of 77,803 showed up to watch the home country skate to a 2-1 victory. The crowd size worked in the Germans' favor for most of the game because of the noise it created. The fans were at their loudest when Felix Schutz scored the winner 21 seconds into overtime.

CHAPTER 40

BIGGEST OVATION

1991 ALL-STAR GAME

BY TIM CAMPBELL

THE PERFECT COLLECTION OF notes, and the emotions they stirred, still resonate long after the day they bounced around the now-demolished Chicago Stadium. Artistry energizes hockey fans, but it was the confluence of that and world events that created an unparalleled memory at the 1991 NHL All-Star Game.

Two days before the Jan. 19, 1991, showcase, a Saturday afternoon affair in the Windy City between the Campbell and Wales Conferences, a 34-country coalition of armed forces endorsed by the United Nations and led by the United States rolled out Operation Desert Storm. Its goal was to expel Iraq from Kuwait to reverse an invasion that had taken place in August 1990.

There was some level of apprehension that the All-Star Game might not or should not be played. The mid-season weekend celebration of the sport, however, went ahead. The player introductions began shortly after noon with a gathering sense that some kind of special occasion was underway.

Its preamble was a standing ovation for an announcement that players would wear UN decals on their helmets to honor the troops. Mindful of that, a moment's silence was requested for servicemen and women, and then, from the perch at the Stadium's east end, Frank Pellico started up that magnificent Barton organ, all 3,663 pipes of it, to accompany a man with some remarkable pipes of his own. The atmosphere had turned solemn, but in the final bars of soloist Wayne Messmer's strong *O Canada*, the cheering began from the crowd of 18,472. And so began the moment that remains so clear for so many people so many years later.

The noise from the three-decked arena rose steadily as Messmer and Pellico took a few note-free seconds to change melodies to *The Star-Spangled Banner*. And with the anthem, that noise kept rising and rising – the singing, the screaming and the roaring, all in concert – going higher and higher to reach full throat.

Boston Bruins right winger Dave Christian, playing in his one and only NHL All-Star Game, stood on the Wales blueline next to Montreal Canadiens goaltender Patrick Roy. The players were stone-still at the bottom of the scene. The combination of the sound and the sights was indeed dazzling. Chicago Stadium was not only decorated for the event, fans also brought and waved their American flags, some of them of flagpole-size, particularly in the upper decks. There were handheld sparklers all about and fan-created signs, such as "The GIs are the real all-stars" and "We support our all-stars in the Gulf," in great supply.

Christian, born in Warroad, Minn., had witnessed firsthand a similar moment some 11 years earlier. He was part of the 'Miracle on Ice' team, which won gold at the 1980 Winter Olympics in Lake Placid, N.Y. For him, the ovation that accompanied the national anthem then has been rivalled only by the feeling he experienced at the 1991 All-Star Game.

"You were just frozen in amazement," Christian said. "I don't know if I had experienced, nor have I since experienced, a national anthem that was that incredible. The rise in the noise level from the start to the end, it literally gave you a chill."

On the opposite blueline, St. Paul, Minn., native Phil Housley, making his fourth of seven All-Star Game appearances, shared Christian's marvel.

"YOU WERE JUST FROZEN IN AMAZEMENT. I DON'T KNOW IF I HAD EXPERIENCED NOR HAVE I SINCE EXPERIENCED A NATIONAL ANTHEM THAT WAS THAT INCREDIBLE. THE RISE IN THE NOISE LEVEL FROM THE START TO THE END, IT LITERALLY GAVE YOU A CHILL"

"The thing I remember most is that national anthem," Housley said. "Chicago's loud anyway, but this was over the top. It was a great feeling to be part of the All-Star Game, but more importantly, being from the U.S. and the cause that was going on, those fans were just unbelievable.

"Mind-blowing, that's how loud it was."

Messmer still attests to that.

"Hear myself? Not so much," he said. "And I could hardly hear the organ. The decibel level was measured up to 110 decibels that day."

The soloist, now in the financial business in the Chicago area, is still performing the anthems at Cubs and Wolves games. But the 42nd All-Star Game will probably never be exceeded, he ventured.

"I remember it as if it were moments ago," Messmer said. "The Gulf War had actually begun and people were more than just a little concerned, because now they were shoot-

BIGGEST OVATION

1991 ALL-STAR GAME

ing real bullets and having them shot back at us. There was a lot of uncertainty and a genuine wave of patriotism for the U.S. and Canada at the time. I knew that this game was one of those great moments where the God-given talent you have and fate were crossing at the same intersection. It was a 'whoa' moment. You knew this was going to be an important one.

"But as my dad used to say, just sing it the way it's supposed to be sung."

The rendition took just a little more than two minutes, in normal time and Stadium anthem tempo. No extra allargando or grandioso (in music terms). Messmer remains proud of that particular performance to this day.

Play-by-play commentator Jim Hughson, who called the game for TSN that afternoon, still wishes he had heard more of it.

"When Wayne started belting out the anthem, well, I didn't hear him," Hughson said. "Chicago was always a good place for the anthem, but never, ever like that. I remember taking off my headset, as I always used to do in the Stadium, just to get a flavor of how

"I KNEW THAT THIS GAME WAS ONE OF THOSE GREAT MOMENTS WHERE THE GOD-GIVEN TALENT YOU HAVE AND FATE WERE CROSSING AT THE SAME INTERSECTION. IT WAS A 'WHOA' MOMENT"

loud the building was and it was absolutely spine-tingling. But I couldn't hear Wayne. I could see him, but couldn't hear him much. That crowd, it just went on and on. It was absolutely numbing, amazing."

The game was won by the Campbell Conference, 11-5. But the details (that Toronto's Vincent Damphousse won the car as game MVP and that the Chicago fans were mighty cranky that their spectacular rookie, Ed Belfour, hadn't been chosen to play) aren't as lasting as how the afternoon began.

Hughson believes it was a watershed moment with Messmer in 1991, further validating the staying power of that performance.

"That day started what we have now, which is spine-tingling anthems at every big NHL event," Hughson said. "And that's all after Wayne Messmer... You can directly link that back to 1991. This one transcended everything."

WAYNE GRETZKY

THE CONTENDERS

MARIO LEMIEUX'S RETURN

Lemieux was at the apex of his career, fresh off back-to-back Stanley Cups and on pace for 200-plus points, when he made a shocking announcement. He'd been diagnosed with Hodgkin's lymphoma, an illness that would require radiation treatment and sideline the 27-year-old for two months. On March 2, 1993, Lemieux completed his final radiation treatment and played that night in Philadelphia, receiving a standing ovation from fans of Pittsburgh's cross-state rival. Incredibly, Lemieux's blazing finish won him the Hart, Art Ross, Ted Lindsay and Bill Masterton Trophies. He led the Penguins to the Presidents' Trophy while posting 2.67 points per game, third-best in NHL history.

50 IN 39

Of all the amazing things accomplished by Wayne Gretzky, one of his earlier moments emerges as one of his most electrifying. On Dec. 30, 1981, as Edmonton was completing a five-game homestand, The Great One had scored four goals on Philadelphia goaltender Pete Peeters in a tight game. Gretzky flipped in the empty-netter with three seconds to play to seal a 7-5 victory for the Oilers over the Flyers, giving him 50 goals in just 39 games to shatter the NHL mark of 50 in 50. On home ice, capping a homestand in which he scored 15 times, "ovation" doesn't begin to describe the pandemonium.

1980 ALL-STAR GAME

On Feb. 5, 1980, 21,002 people packed Joe Louis Arena in Detroit to watch 51-year old Gordie Howe play in his final All-Star Game. At the time, it was the largest crowd ever to watch a hockey game. Howe spent 25 years as a Red Wing and was in his final season after returning to the NHL with the Hartford Whalers, who'd joined league from the World Hockey Association, where Howe had played the previous six seasons. PA announcer John Bell didn't even have to say his name. "And from the Hartford Whalers, representing all of hockey, the greatest statesman for five decades, No. 9!" The standing ovation, which included chants of "Gordie, Gordie, Gordie!" lasted four minutes.

CHAPTER 41

BIGGEST CURSE

MERVYN 'RED' DUTTON

BY STAN FISCHLER

MESSING AROUND WITH MERVYN 'Red' Dutton was never a good idea, whether the challenge was issued on the ice or in the front office. As a defenseman with the Montreal Maroons and later with the New York Americans, Dutton twice led the league in penalties. Nothing the Hall of Famer ever did, however, had the impact of his 48-year curse against the New York Rangers.

Before his hoodoo was ever cast, Dutton retired as a player and became coach, manager and governor of the Americans. Although the Amerks were New York's first NHL team, the Rangers quickly overshadowed them after entering the circuit a year later in 1926-27. A major discrepancy that disturbed Dutton was that his impoverished club had to pay a hefty rent to play in Madison Square Garden while the Rangers, who were owned by MSG, got an eternal freebie. Determined to release his team from the Garden's grasp, Dutton quickly decided the most profitable route was over the Brooklyn Bridge. He planned an arena in downtown Brooklyn precisely where the new Barclays Center will house the New York Islanders in 2015.

"I've always regarded Brooklyn as one of the finest sports centers in the world," Dutton said. "I'm convinced the fans there would be rabid for hockey."

What's more, before 1941-42 began, he changed the team's name to the Brooklyn Americans and completely altered the club's uniforms, featuring a Brooklyn logo across the jersey.

"The response to our planned Brooklyn move has been tremendous," Dutton said. "And if we don't win the Stanley Cup this season, I'll prove myself a real Brooklynite by shouting (the traditional Brooklyn Dodgers war cry), 'Wait 'til next year!' "

Next year never came, but the wait did. Before the season was three months old, the United States had plunged into the Second World War. Steel that was needed for the Brooklyn arena was now earmarked for tanks and guns. No less discouraging was the fact the Amerks lost many key players to the armed forces. In April 1942, Dutton disbanded his club for the duration of the war after obtaining firm promises from the owners of Montreal, Chicago and Detroit that he could revive his franchise when it was over. Those vows looked even better after NHL president Frank Calder died in 1943 and was replaced

“ I LOOKED AROUND THE ROOM AND NOBODY WAS LOOKING AT ME – I GOT THE MESSAGE. ‘GENTLEMEN,’ I SAID TO THE GOVERNORS, ‘YOU CAN STICK YOUR FRANCHISE UP YOUR ASS.’ I GATHERED MY PAPERS AND LEFT ”

by Dutton, who ran the league until 1946 when he resigned to pursue his Brooklyn project. Armed with blueprints, Dutton showed up at the annual governors meeting in 1946, expecting his Amerks to be welcomed back.

“I’ve talked to people in Brooklyn,” Dutton said. “We’ve got a site and $7 million to put up a building as soon as I get the word from here.”

But he got nothing. The Rangers, Maple Leafs and Bruins all vetoed a return of the Amerks, ending Dutton’s dream.

“I looked around the room and nobody was looking at me – I got the message,” Dutton said years later. “ ‘Gentlemen,’ I said to the governors, ‘You can stick your franchise up your ass.’ I gathered my papers and left.”

Soon after, Dutton delivered his deathless curse: as long as he lived, Red vowed in his hoodoo, the Rangers wouldn’t win the Stanley Cup. Dutton delivered the curse in 1946 and died in 1987. The Rangers didn’t win the Cup until 1994.

MERVYN 'RED' DUTTON

THE CONTENDERS

CURSE OF THE BATTED BAT

In Game 3 the 1975 Stanley Cup final between Buffalo and Philadelphia, fog covered the ice due to very warm weather. Suddenly, a bat swooped down, prompting the Sabres' Jim Lorentz to kill it with a swing of his stick. Buffalo lost the series in six games and the loss to the Flyers was blamed on a bad omen brought about by the slaying of an innocent creature. The Sabres came close to the Cup again in 1999, but Brett Hull's toe-in-the-crease overtime goal in Game 6 gave the Dallas Stars the championship. Buffalo is still looking for its first Cup.

CURSE OF SAM LANE

This was a hex put on the Toronto Maple Leafs by a Croatian Canadian whose name was Simon Lauc before he changed it to Sam Lane after immigrating to Canada. Lane had become an ardent Maple Leafs fan when Toronto won three straight Cups in the early 1960s and then a fourth in 1967, all under Punch Imlach. His favorite Leaf, by far, was Frank Mahovlich, the son of Croatian immigrants. Lane was livid when Toronto traded 'Big M' to Detroit and told his son Gary that the Leafs "won't win another Stanley Cup for 50 years" because Mahovlich was traded away. Gary, who spent several years in Los Angeles as a TV writer and producer, wrote a story about the curse in the Dec. 26, 2009, issue of the Toronto *Sun*. As he put it, "If the Leafs don't win the Stanley Cup until then (2018) or later, you can blame my father – and the Leafs management who traded away Mahovlich on March 3, 1968."

CURSE OF WILLIAM PENN

The statue of Philadelphia's most famous son stands atop city hall and, until 1987, municipal policy was that no building could be higher. That year, however, One Liberty Place was built 400 feet taller. As legend has it, Penn cursed the city's sports teams and the Flyers' Stanley Cup bids in '87 and '97 were both shot down. MLB's Phillies broke their part of the hex in 2008, but the Flyers' Cup drought, which began after 1974-75, remains intact.

CHAPTER 42

BIGGEST MYTH

PETE MULDOON

BY RYAN KENNEDY

THE CURSE OF MULDOON is a sore spot in Chicago. So much so that the usually verbose Phil Esposito didn't even want to talk about it. But in a city that still shudders at the mention of the billy goat that haunts baseball's Cubs, Chicago can at least take solace in the fact that Muldoon's hex is long dead.

The origin of the curse was back in 1927, when Chicago owner Major McLaughlin fired Muldoon, the Black Hawks' first coach. As legend has it, Muldoon put an "Irish hex" on the team, defiantly telling McLaughlin the Black Hawks would never end a season in first place. Back in the Original Six era, finishing first was almost as important as winning the Stanley Cup. "That's the thing," said former Hawks defenseman Pat Stapleton. "Over 70 games it was harder to win, right?"

Chicago won the Cup in '34, '38 and '61, but over that period the Hawks failed to claim the Prince of Wales Trophy as the top points earner in the league. In fact, at one point the franchise missed the playoffs in 11 of 12 seasons, finishing last in nine of those 12. In others, Chicago came achingly close, like in 1962-63 when Stan Mikita and Bobby Hull pulled the club within one point of Toronto for first overall.

In 1967, the Hawks finally ended their decades of futility with a whopper of a season, winning the Prince of Wales by 17 points over Montreal and boasting three of the NHL's top four scorers in Mikita, Hull and Kenny Wharram. The Maple Leafs won the Cup that year, but the first-place hex was broken.

Canadian sportswriter Jim Coleman was the authority on the Curse of Muldoon, describing the incident with McLaughlin in broad, cartoonish strokes back in a 1967 column for *Southam News.*

"Accompanied by two leprechauns, the Muldoon strode into the office of Major Frederic McLaughlin," Coleman wrote. "The Muldoon pulled a red crayon from his pocket, drew a mysterious symbol on McLaughlin's expensive wallpaper and intoned these words in a sepulchral voice: 'this team never will finish in first place.' "

As outlandish as it sounds, it was a piece of theater that haunted the franchise for decades, even if the story was a bit foggy to the Hawks themselves.

"Those things are around and you hear about them," Stapleton said. "As a player, some-

> **“THE MULDOON PULLED A RED CRAYON FROM HIS POCKET, DREW A MYSTERIOUS SYMBOL ON MCLAUGHLIN’S EXPENSIVE WALLPAPER AND INTONED THESE WORDS IN A SEPULCHRAL VOICE: ‘THIS TEAM NEVER WILL FINISH IN FIRST PLACE’ ”**

times you don’t even know the story behind them.”

So what finally broke the hex? Muldoon died in 1929, so there was no anniversary to speak of when the Hawks took first in 1967. And it wasn’t even a matter of competition, since the NHL didn’t expand to 12 franchises until the following campaign. The true reason the Curse of Muldoon ended is this: it was never real in the first place.

Coleman, an admitted drinker who had sometimes had problems with deadlines, gave up the ruse years later to author and hockey historian Brian McFarlane. One night Coleman had writer’s block and needed to file his daily column, so he made up the story about Muldoon, assuming people would forget about it in a day or two. Not only did it live on longer than that, even to this day there are Chicago alumni who don’t know the curse was a hoax. That included Stapleton, who only learned of the fraud when told for this book interview in 2013.

“Leave it to Jim, right?” Stapleton said. “God bless him.”

BIGGEST MYTH

PAT STAPLETON

THE CONTENDERS

MIKE MILBURY VS. TOMMY SALO

During a contentious salary arbitration case between the New York Islanders and Salo in 1998, a rumor spread that GM Milbury had ripped into Salo so viciously that the Swedish stopper was reduced to tears. The story was repeated for years whenever the subject of arbitration came up, but Milbury put it to rest when he told The Hockey News it didn't happen. The fable was invented by Salo's agent to gain sympathy for his client.

TARO TSUJIMOTO

Before Japanese goalie Yutaka Fukufuji got into four games with the Los Angeles Kings in 2006-07, there was the legend of Tokyo Katanas center Tsujimoto, drafted 183rd overall by the Buffalo Sabres in 1974. GM Punch Imlach was mocked by his colleagues at the time, because no one had ever heard of the player. At the following training camp, Imlach revealed why: out of boredom, he had invented Tsujimoto out of whole cloth. Although the player never existed, he's still a favorite reference point in Buffalo, even adorning T-shirts and jerseys.

THE PATRICK KANE PUCK

This case has yet to be cracked. Few saw Kane's Stanley Cup-winning goal in real time thanks to a weird angle. Even stranger, however, is what happened after Chicago beat Philadelphia in 2010: no one could find the puck. It's a mystery as to who scooped up Kane's Game 6 biscuit, though linesman Steve Miller is often cited as the last person seen with it.

CHAPTER 43

BIGGEST SCANDAL

DON GALLINGER

BY KEN CAMPBELL

THE WAY YOU'D LIKE to tell this story, Don Gallinger found his peace and died contented and without any lingering resentment or regret. But sometimes the happy ending just doesn't happen. It was that way with Donald Calvin 'Gabby' Gallinger.

Sixty-five years is a lifetime for a lot of people. It has been that long since NHL president Clarence Campbell banned Gallinger and Billy Taylor of the Boston Bruins for life from the NHL for betting on games involving their team. And even after Gallinger and Taylor had their suspensions lifted 22 years later, Gallinger lived out his life a reclusive, bitter man estranged from his family and the hockey world.

At the time of his death in 2000, Gallinger was living in a 10-by-15-foot apartment in Burlington, Ont. His son Don Jr. said his father's living space was crammed with old newspapers and articles about his own hockey career and attempts to have his name cleared. Only about a dozen people showed up to his funeral in his native Port Colborne, Ont. One of them was his childhood friend and Hall of Famer Ted Kennedy. Several business ventures had failed and he wasn't a rich man. His NHL retirement income was $37 a month. His son paid the $8,000 to give his father a dignified burial.

"He died a very lonely person," Don Jr. said. "He was so hurt. He felt much of his life was taken away from him."

Gallinger has two NHL records to his name – one almost nobody remembers and another that will live in infamy. In 1943, Gallinger was 25 days short of his 18th birthday when he scored in overtime to give Boston a 5-4 win over the Montreal Canadiens in the first game of the playoffs, making him the youngest player ever to score an overtime goal in the post-season. (And as long as the NHL has an 18-year-old draft, it's a record that will never be broken.) The other record, of course, he shares with Taylor for the longest suspension in NHL history.

The season was 1947-48 and Gallinger was making $7,500 in his fifth campaign with the Bruins. He'd taken nearly two years off to serve in the Second World War and came back to the NHL to find he was still good enough to play in the league that took him as an underage player because so many players had been lost to the war effort. That was the year Gallinger met Taylor, who'd come to Boston in a trade from the New York Rangers. Gallinger had already bet on the Bruins to win games. But as the story goes, Taylor convinced him he could make $500 to $1,000 a night betting on the Bruins to lose. So they did, but only on games in which they thought the Bruins would lose anyway. They became involved with James Tamer, a Detroit gambler and convicted criminal, and bet on eight games over a period of three months.

One of Gallinger's biggest mistakes was that he denied any wrongdoing and only confessed to his indiscretions after the evidence against him was so insurmountable it couldn't be refuted. It was then that, as Don Jr. remembers, "Clarence Campbell looked my father straight in the eyes and told him he would never play in the NHL again."

Without the protection of a union and with the wrath of Campbell falling upon him, Gallinger was doomed. One thing that irked Gallinger after the fact was that Babe Pratt of the Toronto Maple Leafs was found guilty of gambling on Maple Leafs victories in 1946 and received only a nine-game suspension because he owned up to his misdeeds immediately. Twenty years later, Pratt was inducted into the Hall of Fame.

"HE DIED A VERY LONELY PERSON. HE WAS SO HURT. HE FELT MUCH OF HIS LIFE WAS TAKEN AWAY FROM HIM"

Was Gallinger something of a reprobate? You could probably say so. He left his wife and children in 1962 and had very little to do with his family after that. It was learned later in his life that Gallinger had fathered a son after having an affair with a young Canadian socialite in the 1940s. Prior to leaving his wife and children, he operated several hotels in the Kitchener, Ont., area and made his name as an outstanding baseball player and manager. (Gallinger had been offered contracts by the Boston Red Sox and Philadelphia Phillies while playing with the Bruins and had a tryout with the Red Sox in 1946.)

Perhaps it was the weight of his ban from the NHL that, combined with other things, changed Gallinger. According to his son, the same man who was so chatty and gregarious basically became a recluse in the 1960s. Almost every conversation after that came around to how he had been screwed over by the NHL and especially Campbell. Don Jr. remembered how his father reacted in 1980 when Campbell was convicted of bribing a Canadian senator to lobby on behalf of a company called Sky Shops, in which Campbell was an investor, to continue operating a duty-free concession at the Montreal Airport.

"He said, 'There is this man who is a felon and he made me suffer so much,'" Don Jr. said. "That put a smile on his face."

DON GALLINGER

"CLARENCE CAMPBELL LOOKED MY FATHER STRAIGHT IN THE EYES AND TOLD HIM HE WOULD NEVER PLAY IN THE NHL AGAIN"

Nobody knows how good Gallinger could have been as an NHL player if he hadn't gotten involved in the criminal underbelly of gambling. He was a terrific skater, a heads-up player who could play both ends of the ice and he had a very respectable 65 goals and 153 points in 222 career games when he was banned. It's doubtful he would have followed his childhood pal Kennedy into the Hall of Fame, but he likely would have enjoyed a long and productive career.

"He's 22 years old when this happens and suddenly one year becomes two years becomes five years becomes 10 years," Don Jr. said. "It became a real mental challenge for him because he wanted to clear his name so badly. He did that, but he was never the same."

ALAN EAGLESON

THE CONTENDERS

ALAN EAGLESON

Eagleson was once one of the most powerful men in hockey, but when it all ended for him he was forced to resign his membership in the Hall of Fame and stripped of the Order of Canada, as well as being disbarred by the Law Society of Upper Canada. As the omnipotent executive director of the NHL Players' Association, Eagleson was accused and found guilty of a number of crimes, including skimming profits from international hockey events and defrauding players. He was charged with 34 counts of racketeering, obstruction of justice, embezzlement and fraud in the United States in 1994. He pleaded guilty to mail fraud in Boston and three counts of fraud and embezzlement in Canada later that year.

MIKE DANTON

Estranged from his biological family, the client of a rogue agent and a player who locked horns with Lou Lamoriello, Danton was never far from controversy. But it all went over the top in April 2004 when he was arrested and charged with conspiracy to commit murder and most have assumed the target was his agent, David Frost. How crazy did things get? Well, consider that Danton's original defense lawyer was found not to have a law degree and was charged with two felonies. In July 2004, Danton pleaded guilty to attempting to hire a hitman and was sentenced to seven-and-a-half years in a U.S. prison. He was later transferred to a Canadian prison and granted parole in 2009.

RICK TOCCHET

A nationwide gambling ring is one thing, but a nationwide gambling ring with tentacles that extend to the greatest player in the history of the game is quite another. It all started when a New Jersey state trooper and then-Phoenix Coyotes assistant coach Rick Tocchet were investigated and indicted for their parts in the operation. The state trooper, James Harney, identified Tocchet as a partner and was sentenced to six years in prison. Tocchet pleaded guilty to conspiracy and promoting gambling and was sentenced to two years' probation. Wayne Gretzky, then part-owner and coach of the Coyotes, and his wife, Janet Jones, were investigated but not charged.

CHAPTER 44

BIGGEST TRAGEDY

LOKOMOTIV YAROSLAVL

BY BOB DUFF

MIKE BABCOCK DOESN'T NEED to tell anyone how often he thinks of Ruslan Salei. The Detroit Red Wings coach can show you.

Pulling out his cellphone, Babcock scrolled through photos on it. Finally, he found the one he wanted to share. It was a photo of Salei's No. 24 sweater hanging in a place of dignity in the Belarusian dressing room at the 2012 World Championship.

"That's the way they honored him," Babcock said. "I thought that was spectacular."

Salei, who played for Babcock in Anaheim and Detroit, and former Red Wings assistant coach Brad McCrimmon were among the 44 people who died when the Yakovlev Yak-42 plane carrying the Lokomotiv Yaroslavl team to its opening game of the 2011-12 Continental League season crashed on Sept. 7, 2011.

McCrimmon was just beginning his head coaching career with Lokomotiv. He gave his life pursuing the game he loved, as did every man on the plane that fateful day. Others lost in the accident who were former NHLers included Josef Vasicek, Pavol Demitra, Alexander Karpovtsev, Igor Korolev, Karel Rachunek, Karlis Skrastins and Alexander Vasyunov.

It was a tragedy that touched the lives of all of those in the game, at every level of hockey.

Russian goaltender Nikita Serebryakov of the Ontario League's Saginaw Spirit played with two of the players who died in the crash. One of those he knew well was Alexander Galimov, who survived the crash only to die from injuries in hospital five days later.

"I was hoping that Galimov would survive, but unfortunately he didn't," Serebryakov said. "I was really upset, like everyone else in Russia."

The hockey community is a close-knit one, no matter the nation. Paths cross, bonds form, some last a lifetime. Such as the one that existed between McCrimmon and Nicklas Lidstrom. Their relationship began in 1991 at Joe Louis Arena. One was a grizzled veteran of NHL battles, a farm boy from Saskatchewan. The other was a slick Swede from Vasteras who was about to embark on a career as the best defenseman of his generation. To observers, they might have had the appearance of hockey's version of the *Odd Couple*, but Lidstrom's view of the partnership is more of awe than oddity.

"He was my (defense) partner my first year over here and he was my roommate, too, so I got to know him really well," Lidstrom said. "He wanted to be a head coach. He wanted

to see what it would be like being a head coach in Russia. We all wished him well."

Twenty years earlier, it was McCrimmon who wished Lidstrom well as he made his NHL debut. Detroit GM Bryan Murray acquired McCrimmon from the Calgary Flames, where he'd won a Stanley Cup in 1989, and his veteran presence was a soothing partnership for the learning Lidstrom.

"He was more of a stay-at-home defenseman and that gave me a chance to be part of the offense," Lidstrom said. "He was my partner for every game my first year. He was that steady defenseman who stayed home all the time. He would protect me in situations when things got heated. He was a great partner and I learned a lot from him that first year."

Off the ice, the two lived in the same area, so they carpooled to games. Their wives also bonded and found friendship.

> **"IT STILL BRINGS CHILLS TO EVERYONE. IT'S SOMETHING YOU NEVER THINK COULD EVER HAPPEN. LIFE MOVES ON AND WE NEED TO APPRECIATE ALL THE GOOD TIMES WE HAD WITH THOSE GUYS"**

"He was always happy, always looking at things the positive way," Lidstrom said. "He was always trying to encourage players when things weren't going their way. He helped me out a lot my first year in the league."

A team destroyed, but not eliminated. Lokomotiv took a one-year leave from the KHL, but returned for 2012-13, finishing 16 games over .500. But the memories of those who were lost lingers.

"It still brings chills to everyone," said Detroit defenseman Niklas Kronwall, whose brother Staffan was part of the revitalized Lokomotiv team. "It's something you never think could ever happen. Life moves on and we need to appreciate all the good times we had with those guys. They were all unbelievable guys, on and off the ice. Just great people."

THE CONTENDERS

SWIFT CURRENT BRONCOS

On Dec. 30, 1986, the bus carrying the Western League's Broncos failed to navigate a sharp right bend in snow and freezing rain. It caught black ice and slid off the road, going airborne and rolling onto its side. Four players – Chris Mantyka, Brent Ruff, Scott Kruger and Trent Kresse – were killed. Tim Tisdale, a first-year center with the Broncos that season, recalled an almost serene quietude after the bus skidded to a stop on its right side.

"Nobody panicked, nobody was screaming," he said. "The front window was blown out in the crash and we just crawled out the opening to safety."

It wasn't until the team gathered at Swift Current Union Hospital that they realized not everyone had survived.

"A team is like a family and in tough times, you look out for your family," Tisdale said. "We started taking head counts and we realized there were guys missing. We knew that was bad news."

BILL MASTERTON

Skating across the Oakland Seals blueline before feeding a pass to teammate Wayne Connelly, Minnesota North Stars center Bill Masterton was sandwiched by Seals defenders Ron Harris and Larry Cahan. Falling awkwardly, he struck the back of his head on the ice. He sustained a massive brain injury and died 30 hours later on Jan. 15, 1968, the only on-ice fatality in NHL history.

HOWIE MORENZ

In a race for a loose puck with Chicago's Earl Seibert during a Jan. 28, 1937, game at the old Forum, Montreal's Howie Morenz fell and his skate blade wedged between the boards just as the Black Hawks defenseman slammed into him. Morenz broke his left leg in four places. He announced from his hospital bed that he'd be back next season with the Canadiens as good as new, but the hockey world was stunned when the two-time NHL scoring champion and three-time Hart Trophy-winner died six weeks later from a pulmonary embolism.

BILL MASTERTON

CHAPTER 45

BIGGEST RULE CHANGE

FORWARD PASSING

BY CRAIG BOWLSBY

IN NOVEMBER 1913 SOMETHING happened that changed hockey forever. Frank and Lester Patrick of the Pacific Coast Hockey Association invented a rule called "no offside in centre ice" and thus gave birth to the modern game's first forward pass.

It was hideous.

The hockey world was shocked. For those who experienced it, this new rule changed not only tactics and technique but sportsmanship itself. It had as momentous an impact on the sport as gunpowder did on 14th-century battlefields. But to understand this impact we have to examine what hockey was like before it.

It was perfect.

For 40 years, since the James Creighton era in Montreal, hockey had been honed, stick by stick and rule by rule, into a precise, organized and well-understood game. A team carried one man for each position and the players thought of themselves as "60-minute men" who could play an entire game without a substitute.

Tradition already dictated the game's tactics. A team attacked in a V-shaped flotilla. Within this shape, the puck and the players criss-crossed in confusing patterns. Speed wasn't needed for this part of the game and any player who advanced ahead of the formation was useless. When a man was with the puck he swung into position and when his group was formed he passed the puck backward to a winger or a center, who surged forward and passed it back to another player, who surged forward, and so on, as the flotilla advanced.

However, a player often launched out of the flotilla like a torpedo. Half of the goals scored were by individual attacks when a man would spring out of the pack. Here was where speed finally mattered.

Despite this tradition, the Patrick brothers were never satisfied. Their active, analytical brains constantly examined the possibilities and their new goal was speed. How could they refine the flow and give spectators their biggest thrill? The more they tinkered, the more they felt the energy of the game was writhing in its old form and aching to be released into a new one. Finally, they reached the inescapable conclusion that the only way to release that energy was to break the most sacred of the game's rules. It was a daring experiment.

When the Patricks announced their plans, the hockey world was appalled and confused. Some players hated it, others reserved judgement. Sportswriters and coaches mostly implied that the Patricks were crazy. Even Si Griffis, captain of the Vancouver Millionaires and one of Frank Patrick's key players, called the new rule "impossible."

Passing a puck forward, to the Victorian and Edwardian mind, wasn't only unworkable, it was dishonorable. If one team were steaming out of its own end with the puck, the other team had to have the chance to stop it and to create its own formation to meet the enemy. The forward pass would be so fast and would circumvent the opposing team so easily that it was obviously unfair. It was as if you were on the duelling ground and your enemy suddenly ran over to the side and shot at you.

In addition, players often received penalties for staying ahead of the play and for not getting back "behind the lines" before their own team started out again, whether they touched the puck or not. They called this offense "loafing" and it was considered completely reprehensible. If a player were repeatedly slow at returning (despite the constant puck exchange), he would get a penalty for loafing and everyone would consider him a

“EVEN SI GRIFFIS, CAPTAIN OF THE VANCOUVER MILLIONAIRES AND ONE OF FRANK PATRICK'S KEY PLAYERS, CALLED THE NEW RULE 'IMPOSSIBLE'”

lazy, shiftless and immoral player. And now the Patricks were encouraging and legitimizing this. (Hitting somebody over the head, or breaking his bones, wasn't immoral, even though it might incur a penalty.)

The new rule also made a mockery of the game, because the carefully honed passing sequences – all backward – would no longer have the same importance and significance, at least in the middle of the ice. And hockey in that time was considered a science. The intricate passing was based on geometry, on vectors, on confusing the opponent with rapid permutations and perambulations. If the science could be undone merely by launching the puck forward, then what game were they playing?

Furthermore, how were they supposed to control the puck? The speed of the game, after all, was normally as fast as a player could carry the puck, which would be up to 20 miles an hour. With a forward pass, however, a player could advance the puck at two or three times that rate, or even more, without moving much at all. How was one to handle such an increase in power and speed? There were also many objections about how the new blue lines in the middle of the ice would be used and abused. All of these concerns were valid. But realizing that an entirely new level of hockey was possible, regardless of what form it would take, the Patricks ordered their players to employ the rule no matter what happened and everyone held their breath.

Many unforeseen problems surfaced. A lot more interference happened, since the teammates of the man with the puck often blocked for him as he approached the defensive zone. On the flipside, opponents tended to intercept the puck when it had been sent ahead to the rushing forward. Most importantly, however, the game sped up drastically whenever the forward pass was used and the poor 60-minute men began to gasp and wheeze. They now considered going off for a minute to recuperate, but they got around that in creative ways. They could hide behind the net with the puck to stall. They could create more penalties or delays to give everyone a breather. Or they could just take the puck into their end and signal to the referee that they had to stop the game for a minute. Which the referee did, at least at first.

> **“ONE TORONTO REPORTER SAID IT WAS ‘A GOOD STYLE FOR AN OLD MAN’S GAME, BUT NOT FOR YOUNG MEN WHO HAVE ANY SPEED’”**

And then, almost magically, as if a new language had become unscrambled in their brains, the players began to appreciate and manipulate their new freedom with greater ease. The old bogeyman of loafing evaporated because the center ice play became so fast that there was no time to loaf. Lester Patrick had a love-hate relationship with the new rule, but he found he could use both the new and old systems. He overcame his aversion as a player and, by carefully choosing his moments with the forward passing option, he helped his Victoria Aristocrats win the league title in March 1914.

Then the real test loomed: he took his Victoria team east and played for the Stanley Cup in Toronto. The forward pass was given only one game to prove itself, though, under western rules, and neither team used it well enough to make a decisive difference. Toronto had the better team, with a much hotter goalie, and it defeated Victoria in three straight games, belying the new rule’s importance. The eastern critics still misunderstood the new passing game and saw it as being *slower* than regular hockey. This was partly because the play-

FRANK PATRICK

ers weren't racing back and forth to stay onside, even though the puck actually advanced faster in the center of the ice. One Toronto reporter said it was "a good style for an old man's game, but not for young men who have any speed."

Finally, in 1915, the new weapon was wheeled onto the field and given its true test of fire. The Millionaires had won their league title and met the Ottawa Senators on their home front, at the Georgia Street arena (now called the Denman Arena). The Millionaires used the forward pass as part of their regular game, far more than Lester Patrick's team had done, and they used it to their great advantage. They had immense talent, especially on the attack, while Ottawa was known for its uncrackable defense. Vancouver could use the forward pass in three of the five possible games, but it only needed the first three. The Millionaires blew away the Senators, racing around and through them. They hammered Clint Benedict with shots and with each game they showed how their talent could take flight with great passing. Senators' coach, Alf Smith, fumed that the new rule was "a farce." In the end, Vancouver outscored Ottawa in the three games 26-8.

Nevertheless, the eastern teams still refused to believe their own eyes and lungs, and they hated the need to adapt, even when Seattle used the forward pass to win the Stanley Cup in 1917. The NHL resisted until 1918-19, when it finally gave in and implemented its own forward passing rules, liberating the game from its plodding past and giving it a dynamic future.

HAP HOLMES

THE CONTENDERS

GOALIE FREEDOM

In December 1916, the first goaltenders to receive freedom of movement to stop a goal were those of the PCHA (including the famous Hap Holmes). NHL goalies followed in 1917-18. Before this, they were penalized for going to their knees. When they were allowed to stop the puck any way they could, this revolutionized how goalies played, giving rise to spectacular heroics. Ironically, their goals-against average went *up* in the first year of the rule, as they rushed out of their nets and flopped to the ice too often while challenging attackers. It took a year for goaltenders to get their bearings.

SIX-MAN GAME

The position of rover was the place for players with the greatest skill and creativity. A rover could pivot a team into offensive or defensive mode, or put out fires anywhere on the ice. But when the National Hockey Association officially changed from seven men to six in 1911-12, eliminating the rover, the game opened up and even sped up for every man. This was one of the few times the NHA/NHL discovered an important truth about the game before the PCHA, which only grudgingly accepted the six-man game in 1922.

PENALTY SHOT/SHOOTOUT

Although many other rules have had a greater impact on how hockey is played, the penalty shot has provided one of the most exciting moments of the game. In its slow evolution, the NHA/NHL tried the rule in 1915 and the PCHA introduced it as a regular feature in 1921. It wasn't until 1934, however, that it became an official rule in the NHL. Later, in the '70s and '80s, the riveting shootout nature of the rule was exploited by the NHL in exhibition contests and as its popularity grew it was finally made an official method of resolving tied games in 2005-06.

CHAPTER 46

BIGGEST BRAIN CRAMP

STEVE SMITH

BY WAYNE FISH

NOBODY HAD TO GO to the hospital. Power didn't shut off in the city of Edmonton. No earthquakes, floods or clouds of locusts, either.

But inside Steve Smith's head on the evening of April 30, 1986, things were much worse. The Edmonton Oilers' rookie defenseman was competing in the biggest game of his life – Game 7 of the second round of the playoffs against the Calgary Flames – and had just shot a puck off his own goaltender, Grant Fuhr, into his own net for what turned out to be the deciding goal.

Joe Mullen was sitting on Calgary's bench when the play took place and he still remembers how it all unfolded.

"We dumped the puck in, Fuhr went out to stop it and Steve went back to get it to make a quick outlet pass," Mullen said. "Grant happened to not be back in the net yet. It hit off his leg and went in. It gave us the goal we needed and we went on to win.

"It was like, 'Thank you very much.' It was a hard-fought battle the whole way. That kind of goal can make the difference and it did."

Smith immediately dropped to the ice and covered his head. All he wanted was a chance to make amends. But on that fateful night, after time ran out in the Flames' 3-2 win, he had to take it like a man, even if he did break down in tears in the handshake line. It's a shame that this one play, which happened with 14:46 to play, is what some people remember him for.

"As a team, we shouldn't have been in that situation in the first place," said Smith's teammate Dave Semenko. "It was Game 7 and we still had plenty of time left. It was just one goal."

The play happened on Smith's 23rd birthday, no less. So while people blow out candles on a cake each year and wish for something good, it wouldn't be a stretch to say Smith might wish for something bad to go away. His own goal didn't seal the Stanley Cup for the Flames, who went on to lose in the final to the Montreal Canadiens, but it did cost the Oilers a chance at a third straight championship.

Smith's own goal received so much more attention because it was a Battle of Alberta affair that meant so much to everyone in the province. The Calgary-Edmonton rivalry was

> **“IT WAS LIKE, ‘THANK YOU VERY MUCH.’ IT WAS A HARD-FOUGHT BATTLE THE WHOLE WAY. THAT KIND OF GOAL CAN MAKE THE DIFFERENCE AND IT DID”**

as intense as any in the 1980s at a time when divisional opponents played as many as eight games a season against each other. Mullen believes the play shouldn't define Smith's career. At the time it happened, however, he and his teammates had no sympathy for Smith.

"There wasn't much love lost between the two teams, so I don't think anyone felt bad for him at the time," Mullen said. "Who's to say we wouldn't have won anyway if that hadn't happened? I would think we earned it because we were so close the whole series. It was just unfortunate it came down to one play like that."

Looking back, Semenko agreed with Mullen that there were no sure things for the Oilers if that play hadn't happened.

"There was no guarantee that if we got by Calgary we win the Cup, which might have been our third in a row," Semenko said. "Things were aligned in our favor, but Calgary was always tough. We had to beat them in seven games to win our first Cup (in 1984). This time they had our number."

BIGGEST BRAIN CRAMP

STEVE SMITH

THE CONTENDERS

MARTY MCSORLEY

In 1993, the Los Angeles Kings took Game 1 of the Stanley Cup final against the Canadiens and were leading 2-1 late in Game 2 when Habs coach Jacques Demers called for a measurement on McSorley's stick, which revealed his curve to be illegal. Montreal scored on the resulting power play, won in overtime and cruised to the Cup, taking four straight to win the series 4-1. The Kings finally exorcised the ghosts with their first Cup in 2012.

CHRIS OSGOOD

Osgood is another former NHLer who would like to forget his rookie experience in the playoffs. In the first round against San Jose in 1994, the Detroit goalie attempted to clear a puck and put it right on the stick of the Sharks' Jamie Baker, who promptly deposited it into the Red Wings' wide-open net. That proved to be the winning goal in a 3-2 Game 7 victory. After the game, Osgood wept in his dressing room stall. Like Smith, he would later win three Cups.

MARC BERGEVIN

In Game 2 of a first-round series in 2000, Bergevin, a defenseman for the St. Louis Blues, hand-wrapped a gift for San Jose. With his team on the penalty kill, he caught a deflected pass from the Sharks' Gary Suter in midair with his glove and tried to toss it around his own goal. Bergevin's attempt, however, went right past the glove hand of Blues goaltender Roman Turek and into the St. Louis net, tying the game 1-1. The Sharks, seeded eighth in the Western Conference, went on to win the game and take the series from the Presidents' Trophy-winning Blues.

CHAPTER 47

BIGGEST OVERTIME GOAL

BOBBY ORR

BY BRIAN McNALLY

IT IS THE ICONIC moment of an iconic hockey career. Bobby Orr remains forever in midair, parallel to the ice, arms outstretched, stick raised, screaming with joy after his game-winning overtime goal lifted the Boston Bruins to the 1970 Stanley Cup.

There have been plenty of overtime heroes in NHL history. In reality, Orr's goal simply polished off the underdog St. Louis Blues in a four-game sweep. The series didn't hinge on his simple give-and-go with teammate Derek Sanderson. The famous picture, however, taken by Boston *Record-American* photographer Ray Lussier, lifted the play beyond mere game-winner or Cup-clincher. It perfectly captured one of the greatest players in NHL history at the height of his powers before chronic knee injuries robbed him of those gifts and before contract squabbles led to his ill-fated departure to the Chicago Black Hawks.

Orr was just 22 at the time, but he was already in his fourth full season with Boston. His 33 goals and 120 points in 1969-70 were the start of a six-year stretch better than anything ever put together by an NHL defenseman. That overtime winner was one of nine goals Orr scored in just 14 playoff games that spring as the Bruins won a title for the first time since 1941.

There are dramatic moments that clinch titles or put exclamation points on individual seasons. And then there are those a league uses to sell its sport to the masses, the ones that live forever. There's a reason Orr's goal is repeatedly voted in polls as one of the NHL's greatest. And it's why his opponents that day, even those on the ice for the goal, can look back and smile.

"I was right there," said Blues defenseman Jean-Guy Talbot. "Is it hard to look at that picture? Oh, no. I was proud of it. We were an expansion team playing against Boston. I wasn't feeling too bad. Bobby Orr is the best defenseman who ever played hockey."

Five years later, Orr was essentially finished because of his wrecked knees. More than one writer has compared his talents to a comet flashing across the sky. He played just 36 games after age 27 and retired at 30. The metaphor works because it rings true.

Orr took a risk to score his memorable goal. He jumped up to keep a puck inside the offensive zone early in overtime of Game 4 at Boston Garden. If he whiffed it was easily a 2-on-1 the other way. The Bruins were up 3-0 in the series and the game was tied

BIGGEST OVERTIME GOAL

BOBBY ORR

3-3. Orr skated past St. Louis left winger Larry Keenan along the right boards. From the bottom of the right faceoff circle he passed to Sanderson behind the Blues' goal and immediately pushed toward the front of the net. Talbot reached for Orr, but the pass was already away, so he pivoted toward Sanderson. Too late. There was just enough space in front of the net with defenseman Noel Picard too slow to tie up Orr's stick. The shot was away quickly and it slipped between the pads of St. Louis goalie Glenn Hall. It was off so fast that Orr, tripped by Picard, began his celebration in midair as the home crowd leapt to its feet and roared.

It's all there in the photo. The puck had enough force behind it that it rebounded in and out of the net before Orr even hit the ice. Picard stares back at Orr in despair and Hall hangs from the crossbar to regain his balance, quickly looking away from the Boston celebration in the left corner.

“IT HAPPENED SO FAST AND SUDDENLY THE PUCK IS IN THE NET. THAT WAS THE ONLY PLAYER I DIDN'T WANT TO GET THE PUCK”

Talbot, who won seven Cups with the Montreal Canadiens, later framed a different picture of the play. It's a shot from further down the ice that shows him behind the net, a look of surprise on his face, as Orr remains in the air. For years he kept it at his Quebec home and it's now on display at his son's house in Colorado.

“I framed it,” Talbot said with a laugh. “It was on my wall. Why not? I was playing forward, that's why I was behind the net with Sanderson. It happened so fast and suddenly the puck is in the net. That was the only player I didn't want to get the puck.”

As for Orr, he scored dozens and dozens of prettier goals in his career. This one was so simple: pass the puck, skate to the front of the net and shoot. And in a brilliant career, it was his proudest moment.

BIGGEST OVERTIME GOAL

THE CONTENDERS

SIDNEY CROSBY

Talk about pressure. Canada had pointed for years toward the 2010 Winter Olympics in Vancouver and what mattered more than anything was winning a gold medal in men's hockey. Crosby, seemingly born for the moment, gave it to Canadians with a goal off a feed from Jarome Iginla 7:40 into overtime of the gold medal game against the United States. That 3-2 win came after the Americans had scored to tie the game with just 24.4 seconds left in regulation.

BRETT HULL

A Cup-clinching goal so memorable it led to a rule change. Dallas' Brett Hull was just inside Buffalo goalie Dominik Hasek's crease when he scored in triple overtime of Game 6 in 1999 against the Sabres. That gave the Stars their first title. Under the rules at the time, a player couldn't have his skate inside the blue paint as the puck crossed the goal line or the goal would be disallowed. The exception was if that player already had possession. People in Dallas say Hull did. People in Buffalo still rail against the call. Either way, the NHL tweaked the rule that summer. A player can score within the crease as long as he doesn't interfere with the goalie.

BILL BARILKO

The Toronto defenseman lifted the Maple Leafs to the 1951 Cup with an overtime goal just 2:53 into the extra period of Game 5 against the Montreal Canadiens. It was the fourth Cup in five years for Toronto and Barilko scored it off a mad scramble in the Canadiens' end. Triumph turned to tragedy four months later, though, when Barilko, just 24 and an NHL regular for five seasons, died in a plane crash while on a fishing trip.

CHAPTER 48

BIGGEST CUT

CLINT MALARCHUK

BY AARON PORTZLINE

ALMOST 25 YEARS LATER, Clint Malarchuk is still moved to tears by the memories of that spring night in 1989 when an almost unimaginable scene played out in Buffalo's Memorial Auditorium. The gory injury that day – Malarchuk's throat was cut open by an errant skate blade – sent the veteran goalie's life into a spiral. And it reminded every hockey fan that this sport isn't merely physical and dangerous. It can be, in the worst-case scenario, deadly.

Malarchuk is better now, but the physical wounds healed much quicker than the psychological injuries, the heightened obsessive-compulsive disorder that followed and the resulting post-traumatic stress disorder that nearly took his life through a suicide attempt many years later. Yes, the most horrific injury in the history of professional sports has left its marks.

It happened on March 22, 1989, only two weeks after Malarchuk was traded from the Washington Capitals to the Buffalo Sabres to help them secure a playoff spot. Late in the first period, with St. Louis ahead 1-0, Blues right winger Steve Tuttle and Sabres defenseman Uwe Krupp were pursuing the puck in Buffalo's end when they became entangled and crashed into Malarchuk's net. Tuttle fell backward, his natural reflexes thrusting his legs into the air with a kick. Malarchuk's instinctive reaction was to pull his head back, but that only exposed his neck to Tuttle's skate, which tore across his throat and severed his jugular vein. Blood began spewing from Malarchuk like a garden hose, even as he clasped his hands around his neck to stop it. According to news reports at the time, as many as 11 people in the stands fainted at the sight and two had heart attacks. Three players on the ice vomited.

Malarchuk has relived the scene a million times in his mind and several times publicly.

"I could feel my heart beating and the resulting spurt of blood out of my neck," he said. "I could feel it."

Malarchuk, who was 27 at the time, raced off the ice under his own power, saying he knew his mother was watching on satellite back home in Alberta.

"I didn't want her to see me die on the ice," he said.

Malarchuk believed he was dying and asked an equipment staffer to phone home and tell his mother he loved her. Then he asked for a priest. Malarchuk credited Sabres trainer Jim Pizzutelli, an United States Army medic during the Vietnam War, with saving his life, by literally putting his hands "in my neck" and squeezing his carotid artery to stanch the bleeding. Still, Malarchuk was estimated to have lost a third of his blood.

The configuration of the 'Aud' may have saved Malarchuk's life. Rather than access the dressing room from behind the bench like most buildings, the Sabres used a door in one corner of the rink, which just happened to be the end in which Malarchuk was playing.

"If I had to go even that much farther, it's a different story," Malarchuk said. "And if it had been the second period – when we were on the other end of the ice – I'd be a goner."

Doctors told Malarchuk if the cut had occurred one-eighth of an inch higher on his neck or one-eighth of an inch deeper, he likely would have died on the ice. Remarkably, after enduring multiple surgeries throughout the evening on his neck, throat, jugular vein and carotid artery, Malarchuk spent just one day in the hospital. He played for the Sabres 11 days later, returning to a standing ovation in a relief appearance with five minutes remaining in the season finale.

"I COULD FEEL MY HEART BEATING AND THE RESULTING SPURT OF BLOOD OUT OF MY NECK. I COULD FEEL IT"

But Malarchuk didn't truly overcome the injury for many years.

He credited his obsessive-compulsive disorder with giving him the work ethic necessary to forge a 10-year NHL career. Growing up in Grand Prairie, Alta., Malarchuk would spend several hours in an empty rink after practice working on leg drills and side-to-side motions to quicken his pads. The OCD began to emerge in different ways, however, leading to public scrapes and alcohol-fuelled rages in later years.

Nearly 20 years after Malarchuk's gruesome injury in the same city, Florida Panthers right winger Richard Zednik suffered a severe skate laceration to the side of his neck. The accident brought Malarchuk's incident back to the foreground. Malarchuk began spiralling, his drinking picking up and his isolation taking hold.

Eight months after Zednik's injury put Malarchuk back in the media spotlight, his wife, Joanie, found him on their ranch in Reno, Nev., and witnessed him fire a bullet into his skull, shattering his chin, teeth, cheekbone and eye socket. Malarchuk has since been diagnosed with post-traumatic stress disorder, all tied to that night in Buffalo when he nearly became the NHL's second on-ice fatality. Now he's the goaltending coach of the Calgary Flames and gives speeches throughout Canada on overcoming the stigmas of mental disorders.

BIGGEST CUT

CLINT MALARCHUK

THE CONTENDERS

RICHARD ZEDNIK

On Feb. 10, 2008, Buffalo was once again the site of a nasty skate-to-the-neck incident. Zednik was clipped along the side of his neck by Panthers teammate Olli Jokinen in a game against the Sabres. Zednik sustained a sliced carotid artery, but his jugular – unlike Malarchuk's – wasn't cut. Also unlike Malarchuk, Zednik took plenty of time to recover. He didn't play until the following season.

BORJE SALMING

Salming may have forever debunked the myth that Swedes aren't tough enough to thrive in the NHL. If his play didn't do it – it should have – the gruesome injury the Toronto Maple Leafs defenseman sustained in 1986 from the skate blade of the Detroit Red Wings' Gerard Gallant sure must have. After falling in front of the net, Salming was sliced from forehead to mouth, the cut weaving just between his right eye and nose. More than 200 stitches were needed to close it.

KRIS DRAPER

In the 1996 Western Conference final, Colorado's Claude Lemieux demolished the unsuspecting Detroit center Kris Draper from behind, slamming him face-first into the boards next to the Red Wings' bench. Draper suffered a broken jaw, a broken nose, a fractured cheekbone, a concussion and several cracked teeth. Lemieux was given only a two-game suspension. The Avalanche went on to win that series and sweep the Panthers to win the Stanley Cup, but the rivalry between Colorado and Detroit thrived for more than a decade.

CHAPTER 49

BIGGEST CAJONES

TED LINDSAY

BY BOB DUFF

TO THIS DAY, TED Lindsay doesn't consider his actions brave or heroic. Actually, he remains uncertain of the motivation for his bid to launch the NHL Players' Association in the mid-1950s.

"Don't ask me why I did it," Lindsay said. "The Lord didn't come down and say, 'Ted, you're one of the better players in hockey today. Somebody like you has to do this.' "

The attempt eventually failed, but that Lindsay did it at all speaks volumes about his character and courage.

"The NHL was a dictatorship," he said. "When you signed your contract, if you had an agent or a lawyer, they sent you home. They said, 'Good luck to you, son. We hope you have a good life.' They had us where they wanted us. I just wanted to give us a voice. We had no voice."

On Feb. 11, 1957, Lindsay, a left winger with the Detroit Red Wings, was announced as president of the newly formed NHLPA.

"Actually, we don't have many grievances," Lindsay said at the time. "We just felt we should have an organization of this kind. We're not looking for any trouble."

What the players were looking for was a better deal with the NHL's pension plan. Montreal's Doug Harvey, Chicago's Gus Mortson and Boston's Fern Flaman were named vice-presidents. Toronto's Jim Thomson was named secretary and New York's Bill Gadsby treasurer. Organizing this group was no easy feat, though. Owners met regularly every season, but players never spoke to each other, according to Lindsay, who was spoken to the least, in civil terms, of all the players in the league. Known as 'Scarface' and 'Terrible Ted,' Lindsay asked no quarter and gave none between the boards.

"Things were different back then," he said. "Hockey players were so competitive. They hated every member of every other team."

Lindsay acquired the services of Lewis & Mound, the same law firm that helped MLB players establish their association. The goal at the time wasn't to begin collective bargaining, but merely to allow players more freedom when negotiating their own contracts. Ultimately, the owners quashed this attempt at labor organization and then exacted revenge on those behind the NHLPA. In the summer of 1957, after posting a career-high

TED LINDSAY

85 points, Lindsay was dealt to the Black Hawks by Red Wings GM Jack Adams. Thomson was traded to Chicago for cash, Mortson was shipped to Detroit and Gadsby (Detroit) and Harvey (New York) were also dealt in 1961. Flaman was sent to the minors.

"Lindsay has been paying too much attention to outside business interests," Adams said, "and not enough to hockey."

Naturally, Lindsay viewed things differently.

"I had my best year as a Red Wing the year that I got traded," he said. "I was traded because of the association. I know Jack Adams turned every player on the team against me, one by one."

Current members of the NHLPA recognized Lindsay's efforts in 2010, when they renamed the trophy they present annually to their best player the Ted Lindsay Award.

"All NHL players, current and former, owe a great deal of gratitude to Ted for his efforts," said Jarome Iginla.

During a career in which Lindsay took on all comers, taking on those who ran the game was his gutsiest fight.

"I'd do the same thing today," he said. "I believe in doing the right thing."

THE CONTENDERS

EDDIE SHORE

The eccentric four-time Hart Trophy-winning Bruins defenseman entered Boston Garden on game night wearing a matador's cape while the band played *Hail to the Chief*. And once, while receiving stitches to his ear, Shore asked the attending doctor for a mirror to ensure the physician was sewing him up properly.

ALEXANDER MOGILNY

Mogilny's defection to the United States was the stuff of spy movies. He became the first Soviet player to defect for the U.S. after contriving a plan with the Buffalo Sabres to get him to the United States following the 1989 World Championship in Sweden. Mogilny was just 17 at the time. Others followed similar paths until the 1990s when the collapse of the Soviet Union paved the way for Russians to play freely in the NHL.

PAUL MULVEY

The Los Angeles Kings were playing the Vancouver Canucks on Jan. 24, 1982, when a fight broke out. Kings coach Don Perry ordered tough guy Mulvey to leave the bench and join the fray, but he refused. A week later, he was in the minors.

"I'm not going to be a designated assassin and come off the bench and fight," Mulvey said at the time. Within a year, he was out of hockey.

CHAPTER 50

BIGGEST SHOT

ZDENO CHARA

BY MIKE LOFTUS

THE BOSTON BRUINS HAVE had six straight playoff berths through 2013, made two Stanley Cup final appearances in three years and won a Cup in 2011. So a player isn't likely to complain about joining the B's these days. There's also a big bonus: playing for the Bruins means not having to square up to or slide in front of the terrifying shot of their captain, Zdeno Chara.

Well, on purpose, anyway. Dallas Stars center Rich Peverley, who spent two-plus seasons with the Bruins after they obtained him from the Atlanta Thrashers at the 2011 trade deadline, found out the accidental occupational hazards of being Chara's teammate.

"First game after I got traded to Boston, I got hit with one of 'Z's' shots in the back of the leg," Peverley said. "Oh, man."

Fortunately, Peverley wasn't hit by one of Chara's record-breaking blasts. And whenever the NHL can fit an all-star weekend into its schedule, Chara seems to launch one.

The 6-foot-9, 255-pound defenseman owns the NHL's biggest shot. He won five straight hardest shot competitions (an unmatched run from 2008 to 2012) setting a record in each of the last three. Until the league's next All-Star Game, hosted by the Columbus Blue Jackets in 2015, Chara's rocket of 108.8 miles per hour at Scotiabank Place in Ottawa in 2012 will stand as the fastest on record.

The mark may not be safe, though.

"It's always my motto: I want to be better every season," Chara said after he set the record.

That's bad news for opponents, because as long as Chara continues to get so much velocity on his shots, those in their path aren't safe. Since he's under pressure and has to control a pass or one-time a moving puck, Chara probably isn't crushing shots under game conditions that travel as fast as his record-breakers – 105.4 mph in 2009, 105.9 in 2011 and the crazy 108.8 in 2012 – but they're plenty hard enough. Just ask Jay Pandolfo, a longtime opponent of Chara's with the New Jersey Devils and New York Islanders who got to spend 2012-13 with him in Boston.

"I've been hit by his shot," Pandolfo said. "But I've been fortunate. He hasn't broken anything on me yet, but I know he's broken bones on other guys."

Added defenseman Wade Redden, Chara's teammate with the Ottawa Senators and Bru-

BIGGEST SHOT

ZDENO CHARA

ins: "I'm still standing here, so he must never have hit me with one. But when I was with the Rangers, I know Ryan Callahan broke an ankle when he got hit by Z's shot."

Callahan was, in fact, lost for the remainder of the regular season and playoffs in 2011 after bravely, if unadvisedly, getting in front of a Chara shot on April 4.

Shot blocking is an accepted part of life in the NHL, but when Chara is doing the shooting it's the ultimate risk. Although he uses an exceptionally stiff shaft on a stick that exceeds the standard maximum length of 63 inches (the NHL allows it because of his height), Chara can rightly claim to have the league's fastest shot. He's not the only NHLer who can crank pucks at speeds above 100 mph, but his shot is different.

"There are guys who shoot the puck and it just kind of zings in," Redden said. "With Z, it's almost like a 10-pound weight coming off his stick. It's just such a heavy shot. I remember the goalies in Ottawa doing warmup drills, when Z would only take a half-slapper. They'd still be wincing after catching it."

"I'VE BEEN HIT BY HIS SHOT. BUT I'VE BEEN FORTUNATE. HE HASN'T BROKEN ANYTHING ON ME YET, BUT I KNOW HE'S BROKEN BONES ON OTHER GUYS"

In game conditions, teams do what they can to stick close to Chara when the Bruins have the puck in the offensive zone. That way, he doesn't have time to take a full wind-up or, even better, time to shoot at all. In hardest shot competitions, however, where he's allowed to get a running start and crush a puck that's lying perfectly still and flat, Chara is deadly.

Dramatic, too, on occasion. In the 2011 competition at Raleigh, N.C., Shea Weber of the Nashville Predators actually had a harder shot (104.8 mph) than Chara did (104.1) in preliminaries, but when they squared off in the final round Chara put up a then-record 105.9, while Weber dropped to 103.4. Weber also topped Chara's 105.9 in 2012 by hitting 106 on the radar gun, but Chara's 108.8 later in the competition blew that shot away.

"Will I ever win?" Weber joked. "Not while he's around."

THE CONTENDERS

AL MACINNIS

He earned a Stanley Cup, Conn Smythe Trophy, Norris Trophy, Olympic gold medal, four first-team all-star berths and a league-record seven hardest shot competitions. The Hall of Famer barely topped 100 mph (his 100.4 mph cannon in 1998 was his best winning shot) during his career, but MacInnis didn't play in the era of feather-light composite sticks. He was dominant throughout the 1990s, winning for the first time in 1991, adding a run of four straight titles starting in 1997 and winning as late as 2003.

AL IAFRATE

Skeptics suggest that Iafrate's winning shot of 105.2 mph in 1993 had to be the result of a radar gun error, because it took Chara until 2009 to knock it from the top of the chart. But there was no debating that the charismatic, reckless and altogether unique defenseman was among his era's hardest shooters. Iafrate always gave MacInnis a run for his money, winning the very first competition in 1990 (his winning shot travelled at 96 mph) and doing it again in '93 and '94.

SHEA WEBER

Unless he gets another crack at Chara, Weber will stand as the hardest shooter never to win a title. But he can claim something Chara can't: a 20-goal season. Weber pumped in 23 in 2008-09, while Chara topped out at 19 that same season. Weber can also bring the heat during game action. During the 2010 Winter Olympics in Vancouver, he sizzled a clapper past Germany's Thomas Greiss that went straight through the mesh.

PHOTO CREDITS

8	PHIL ELLSWORTH/NHLI VIA GETTY IMAGES
11	DAVE SANDFORD/NHLI VIA GETTY IMAGES
13	JEN FULLER/GETTY IMAGES
15	GRAIG ABEL/NHLI VIA GETTY IMAGES
16	FRANK PRAZAK/HHOF IMAGES
20	ROBERT LABERGE/ALLSPORT
22	MELCHIOR DIGIACOMO/GETTY IMAGES
26	NEW YORK TIMES CO./GETTY IMAGES
29	BRUCE BENNETT STUDIOS/GETTY IMAGES
31	BRUCE BENNETT STUDIOS/GETTY IMAGES
34	GRAIG ABEL/NHLI VIA GETTY IMAGES
36	JIM MCISAAC/GETTY IMAGES
37	BRUCE BENNETT STUDIOS/GETTY IMAGES
39	JOHN RUSSELL/NHLI VIA GETTY IMAGES
40	DON SMITH/NHLI VIA GETTY IMAGES
42	JEFF VINNICK/GETTY IMAGES/NHLI
43	MICHAEL MARTIN/NHLI VIA GETTY IMAGES
46	ANDRE RINGUETTE/GETTY IMAGES
48	JONATHAN NACKSTRAND/AFP/GETTY IMAGES
51	JOHN WOODS/WINNIPEG FREE PRESS
53	GETTY IMAGES
55	BRUCE BENNETT STUDIOS/GETTY IMAGES
58	GLENN CRATTY/ALLSPORT
59	ALLSPORT/ALLSPORT
61	STEVE BABINEAU/NHLI VIA GETTY IMAGES
62	BRUCE BENNETT STUDIOS/GETTY IMAGES
66	B BENNETT/GETTY IMAGES
68	JUSTIN K. ALLER/GETTY IMAGES
71	HHOF IMAGES
73	BRUCE BENNETT STUDIOS/GETTY IMAGES
75	HARRY SCULL/ALLSPORT
76	BRUCE BENNETT STUDIOS/GETTY IMAGES
79	BRUCE BENNETT STUDIOS/GETTY IMAGES
83	DENIS BRODEUR/NHLI VIA GETTY IMAGES
85	BRUCE BENNETT STUDIOS/GETTY IMAGES
87	B BENNETT/GETTY IMAGES
90	HHOF IMAGES
93	B BENNETT/GETTY IMAGES
95	GREGG FORWERCK/NHLI VIA GETTY IMAGES
97	JIM MCISAAC/GETTY IMAGES
100	BRUCE BENNETT STUDIOS/GETTY IMAGES
101	AL BELLO/GETTY IMAGES/NHLI
103	BRUCE BENNETT/GETTY IMAGES
105	SCOTT AUDETTE/NHLI VIA GETTY IMAGES
108	BRIAN BABINEAU/NHLI VIA GETTY IMAGES
109	JEFF GROSS/GETTY IMAGES
111	MIKE STOBE/NHLI VIA GETTY IMAGES
112	PAUL BERESWILL/GETTY IMAGES

PHOTO CREDITS

113	JOE SARGENT/NHLI VIA GETTY IMAGES
117	PATRICK MCDERMOTT/GETTY IMAGES
119	CHRISTIAN PETERSEN/GETTY IMAGES
121	BRUCE BENNETT STUDIOS/GETTY IMAGES
123	RICK STEWART/GETTY IMAGES
125	BRUCE BENNETT STUDIOS/GETTY IMAGES
127	BRUCE BENNETT STUDIOS/GETTY IMAGES
130	THN ARCHIVES
135	DENIS BRODEUR/NHLI VIA GETTY IMAGES
138	BRIAN BABINEAU/NHLI VIA GETTY IMAGES
140	CHARLES HOFF/NY DAILY NEWS ARCHIVE VIA GETTY IMAGES
141	JIM MCISAAC/GETTY IMAGES
143	BRUCE BENNETT STUDIOS/GETTY IMAGES
144	DENIS BRODEUR/NHLI VIA GETTY IMAGES
147	THN ARCHIVES
148	B BENNETT/GETTY IMAGES
150	NAT TUROFSKY/HHOF IMAGES
153	BRIAN BABINEAU/NHLI VIA GETTY IMAGES
155	BRUCE BENNETT STUDIOS/GETTY IMAGES
159	ADRIAN DENNIS/AFP/GETTY IMAGES
162	BRIAN BABINEAU/NHLI VIA GETTY IMAGES
166	DAVE SANDFORD/GETTY IMAGES
168	MELCHIOR DIGIACOMO/GETTY IMAGES
171	ROBERT SULLIVAN/AFP/GETTY IMAGES
173	ROBERT SULLIVAN/AFP/GETTY IMAGES
174	BRUCE BENNETT/GETTY IMAGES
177	LEON HALIP/GETTY IMAGES
179	GREGORY SHAMUS/NHLI VIA GETTY IMAGES
183	BRUCE BENNETT STUDIOS/GETTY IMAGES
185	FOCUS ON SPORT/GETTY IMAGES
189	B BENNETT/GETTY IMAGES
193	FRANK PRAZAK/HHOF IMAGES
194	NO PHOTO CREDIT
197	NAT TUROFSKY/HHOF IMAGES
199	B BENNETT/GETTY IMAGES
202	YURY KUZMIN/KHL PHOTO AGENCY VIA GETTY IMAGES
205	B BENNETT/GETTY IMAGES
209	UNKNOWN/HHOF IMAGES
211	UNKNOWN/HHOF IMAGES
215	BRUCE BENNETT STUDIOS/GETTY IMAGES
216	ART FOXALL/GETTY IMAGES
218	BRUCE BENNETT STUDIOS/GETTY IMAGES
221	ELSA HASCH/ALLSPORT
225	B BENNETT/GETTY IMAGES
226	ELIOT J. SCHECHTER/NHLI VIA GETTY IMAGES
228	BRUCE BENNETT STUDIOS/GETTY IMAGES
231	BRIAN BABINEAU/NHLI VIA GETTY IMAGES
233	VICTOR DECOLONGON/GETTY IMAGES

ACKNOWLEDGMENTS

One name appears on the cover, but the Biggest of Everything in Hockey *was truly a team effort. Thanks abound.*

To…

- The Hockey News' editor in chief, Jason Kay, for entrusting me with all the responsibilities, big and small, that came with putting this book together.
- Edward Fraser, THN's managing editor, for helping me handle the perils and avoid the pitfalls of being a first-time book editor.
- Luke Sawczak, for his attention to the dirtiest details of proofreading.
- THN staffers Rory Boylen, Ken Campbell, Brian Costello, Ryan Kennedy, Matt Larkin and Adam Proteau, for weaving some of the book's best yarns.
- Freelancers Craig Bowlsby, Tim Campbell, Kyle Cicerella, Adrian Dater, Bob Duff, Stan Fischler, Wayne Fish, Jay Greenberg, Geoff Kirbyson, Mike Loftus, Sarah McLellan, Brian McNally, Aaron Portzline, Rob Riches, Taylor Rocca and Michael Traikos, for lending their expertise and filling in holes.
- Hockey historians, fans, media types and especially GMs, coaches and players (past and present), for taking to the time to talk.
- Erika Vanderveer, THN's art director, for making all this bigness look beautiful.
- The management team of THN publisher, Caroline Andrews, book publisher Marc Laberge and associate book publisher, Susan Antonacci, for their work behind the scenes.
- The members of the marketing/communications department, Tracey Finkelstein, Carlie McGhee, Erin Quinn and Alyson Young, for helping to get the word out.
- Fact-checkers extraordinaire, Lindsay Collicot and Casey Ippolito, who get the biggest shout-outs for sweating all the small stuff about hockey's biggest.